Goethe's World View

by Rudolf Steiner

MERCURY PRESS

This edition of *Goethe's World View*
is a translation by William Lindeman from
Goethes Weltanschauung, published by
Verlag der Rudolf Steiner Nachlassverwaltung
Dornach, Switzerland, 1963.

Cover: Graphic form by Rudolf Steiner
(originally as a study for the book *Truth and Science)*
Layout and lettering by Peter Stebbing.

ISBN 978-1-957569-24-6

Copyright © 1985, 2023 by Mercury Press

MERCURY PRESS
an imprint of SteinerBooks
834 Main Street, PO Box 358
Spencertown, New York 12165
www.steinerbooks.org

Contents

Preface to the New Edition, 1918 1
Preface to the First Edition, 1897 2
Introduction 7

I.
Goethe's Place in the Development of Western Thought

Goethe and Schiller 10
The Platonic World View 14
The Consequences of the Platonic World View 21
Goethe and the Platonic World View 31
Personality and World View 45
The Metamorphosis of World Phenomena 57

II.
Goethe's View on the Nature and Development of Living Beings

Metamorphosis 74

III.
The Contemplation of the World of Colors

The Phenomena of the World of Colors 117

IV.
Thoughts about the Developmental History of the Phenomena of Earth and Air

Thoughts about the Developmental History of the Earth 142
Observations about Atmospheric Phenomena 148

V.
Goethe and Hegel 151

Epilogue to the New Edition of 1918 155

Preface to the New Edition, 1918

In 1897 I undertook to describe in this book the Goethean world view. I wanted to draw together what the study of the Goethean spiritual life over the course of many years had given me. The "Preface to the First Edition" gives a picture of what I felt my goal to be back then. Were I writing this preface today I would not write it any differently with respect to content but only with respect to style. But since I see no reason to change anything essential in the rest of the book, it would seem to me dishonest to take a different tone today in speaking about the feelings with which I sent the book into the world twenty years ago. Neither what I have been able to follow in the Goethe literature since its publication nor the findings presented by recent natural scientific research have changed the thoughts I expressed in the book. I believe I am not without understanding for the great advances of this research in the last twenty years. But I do not believe that it gives any reason to speak differently at present about Goethe's world view than I did in 1897. What I said about the relationship of the Goethean world view to the situation then with respect to the generally accepted ideas about nature also seems valid to me with respect to the natural science of our day. The stance of my book would not be any different had I written it today. Only some additions and expansions that seemed important to me in many places distinguish this new edition from the old one.

In the epilogue to this new edition I have expressed the fact that what I have published in the last sixteen years about spiritual science also cannot cause me to make any essential change in content.

Rudolf Steiner

Preface to the First Edition

The thoughts which I express in this book are meant to contain the fundamental elements that I have observed in Goethe's world view. In the course of many years I have contemplated the picture of this world view again and again. There was a particular appeal for me in looking upon what nature had revealed of its being and laws to Goethe's refined organs of sense and spirit. I learned to understand why Goethe experienced these revelations as a good fortune and happiness so great that he sometimes valued them more highly than his poetic gift. I lived into the feelings which moved through Goethe's soul when he said that "nothing motivates us so much to think about ourselves as when, after a long interval, we finally see again objects of the highest significance, scenes of nature with particularly decisive characteristics, and compare the impression remaining from the past with the present effect. We will then notice by and large that the object emerges more and more, that, while we earlier experienced joy and suffering in our encounter with the objects and projected our happiness and perplexity onto them, we now, with egoism tamed, grant them their rightful due, which is that we recognize their particularities and learn to value their characteristics more highly by thus living into them. The artistic eye yields the first kind of contemplation; the second kind is suited to the researcher of nature; and I had to count myself, although at first not without pain, still in the end fortunate that, as the first kind of sense threatened to leave me by and by, the second kind developed all the more powerfully in eye and spirit."

One must be acquainted with the impressions that Goethe received from the phenomena of nature if one wants to understand the full content of his poetic works. The secrets he gleaned from the being and becoming of the creation live in his artistic productions and are revealed only to someone who gives heed to the communications that the poet makes about nature. A person cannot dive down into the depths of Goethean art to whom Goethe's observations of nature are unknown.

Feelings such as these impelled me to occupy myself with Goethe's nature studies. They allowed first of all the ideas to ripen, which more than ten years ago I communicated in Kuerschner's *Deutscher Nationalliteratur*. What I began back then in the first volume I have developed more fully in the three following volumes of the scientific writings of Goethe, of which the last one is appearing just at this time. The same feelings guided me as I undertook some years ago the wonderful task of being responsible for a part of the natural scientific writings of Goethe for the comprehensive Weimar edition of Goethe's works. What I brought to this work in the way of thoughts, and the thoughts that arose in me during it, form the content of the present book. I can characterize this content as *experienced* in the fullest sense of the word. I have sought to draw near to the ideas of Goethe from many starting points. I have called up all the opposition slumbering in me to Goethe's way of looking at things in order to safeguard my own individuality in the face of the power of this unique personality. And the more I developed my own world view, won for myself, the more I believed I understood Goethe. I tried to find a light that would even illuminate the places in Goethe's soul that remained dark to himself. Between the lines of his works I wanted to read what would make him entirely comprehensible to me. The powers of his spirit, which governed him but of which he did not himself become conscious, these I sought to discover. I wanted to see into the essential character traits of his soul.

When it is a matter of considering a personality psychologically, our age loves to leave its ideas in a kind of mystical semi-darkness. Clarity of thought in such things is held in contempt today as dry intellectual knowledge. It is believed that one can penetrate more deeply if one speaks about one-sidedly mystical abysses of soul life, about demonic powers within the personality. I must admit that this enthusiasm for a misguided mystical psychology appears to me as superficiality. It is present in people in whom the content of the world of ideas arouses no feelings. They cannot descend into the depths of this content. They do not feel the warmth that streams forth from it. Therefore they seek this warmth in unclarity. Whoever is capable of living into the bright spheres of the world of pure thoughts feels within him something that he cannot feel anywhere else. One can come to know personalities like that of Goethe only if one is able to take up into oneself, in all their light-filled clarity, the ideas by which such personalities are governed. A person who loves a false mysticism in psychology will perhaps find my way of looking at things cold. But is it my fault that I cannot regard what is dark and indefinite as one and the same with what is profound? I sought to present the ideas that held sway in Goethe as active powers just as purely and clearly as they appeared to me. Perhaps many will also find the lines I have drawn, the colors I have applied, too simple. I believe, however, that one best characterizes what is great if one tries to present it in all its monumental simplicity. The little adornments and appendages only confuse one's contemplation. It is not the incidental thoughts, to which this or that less significant experience moved Goethe, that are important to me about him, but rather the basic direction of his spirit. Although this spirit does also take side paths here and there, *one* main tendency is always recognizable. And this is what I have sought to follow. If someone believes that the regions through which I have gone are ice-cold, I believe of him that he has left his *heart* at home. If someone wants to reproach me by saying that I portray only those aspects of the Goethean world view to which my own thinking and feeling direct me, then I can only respond that I want to look upon another personality only in the way that he must appear to me according to my own being.

I do not value very highly the *objectivity* of those portrayers who want to deny themselves when they present the ideas of others. I believe that this objectivity can paint only dull and pallid pictures. A battle underlies every true presentation of another's world view, and someone who is fully conquered will not be the best portrayer. The other's power must compel my respect, but my own weapons must perform their service. I have therefore stated without reserve that in my view the Goethean way of thinking has its limit, that there are regions of knowledge which remain closed to it. I have shown which direction the observation of world phenomena must take if it wants to penetrate into regions that Goethe did not enter upon, or in which, when he did go into them, he wandered about uncertainly. As interesting as it may be to follow a great spirit upon his path, I want to follow each one only as far as he benefits me myself. For it is not the contemplation, the knowledge, that is valuable, but rather the life, one's own activity. The pure historian is weak, is not a powerful man. Historical knowledge robs one of the energy and spring of one's own activity. Whoever wants to understand everything will not be much himself. What is fruitful is alone true, Goethe has said. Insofar as Goethe is fruitful for our time, one ought to live into his world of thoughts and feelings. And I believe that there will emerge from the following presentation the fact that innumerable treasures lie hidden within this world of thoughts and feelings that have not yet been raised. I have indicated the places where modern science has not kept up with Goethe. I have spoken of the poverty of our present-day world of ideas and contrasted to it the wealth and fullness of the Goethean one. In Goethe's thinking there are seeds that modern science should bring to fruition. This thinking could be an example for science. Science has more material from observations than Goethe had, but it has permeated this material only with a meager and insufficient content of ideas. I hope that there will emerge from my book how little the modern natural scientific way of thinking is in a position to criticize Goethe and how much it could learn from him.

Rudolf Steiner

Introduction

If one wants to understand Goethe's world view, one cannot content oneself with listening to what he himself says about it in individual statements. To express the core of his being in crystal-clear, sharply stamped sentences did not lie in his nature. Such sentences seemed to him rather to distort reality than to portray it rightly. He had a certain aversion to holding fast, in a transparent thought, what is alive, reality. His inner life, his relationship to the outer world, his observations about things and events were too rich, too filled with delicate components, with intimate elements, to be brought by him himself into simple formulas. He expresses himself when this or that experience moves him to do so. But he always says too much or too little. His lively involvement with everything that comes his way causes him often to use sharper expressions than his total nature demands. It misleads him just as often into expressing himself indistinctly where his nature could force him into a definite opinion. He is always uneasy when it is a matter of deciding between two views. He does not want to rob himself of an open mind by giving his thoughts an incisive direction. He reassures himself with the thought that "the human being is not born to solve the problems of the world but is, indeed, born to seek where the problem begins, and then to keep himself within the limits of what is comprehensible." A problem that the person believes he has solved takes away from him the possibility of seeing clearly a thousand things that fall into the domain of this problem. He is no longer attentive to them, because he believes himself to be enlightened about the region into which they fall. Goethe would rather have two opposing opinions about an issue than *one* definite one. For each thing seems to him to comprise an infinitude, which one must approach from different sides in order to perceive something of its entire fullness. "It is said that the truth lies midway between two opposing opinions. Not at all! It is the problem that lies between, the invisible, the eternally active life, thought of as at rest." Goethe wants to keep his thoughts alive so that he could transform them at any moment, if reality should induce him to do so. He does not want to be right; he wants always "to be going after what is right." At two different points in time he expresses himself differently about the same thing. A rigid theory, which wants once and for all to bring to expression the lawfulness of a series of phenomena, is suspect to him, because such a theory takes away from our power of knowledge its unbiased relationship to a mobile reality.

If, in spite of this, one wants to have an overview of the unity of his perceptions, then one must listen less to his words and look more to the way he leads his life. One must be attentive to his relationship to things when he investigates their nature and in doing so add what he himself does not say. One must enter into the most inward part of his personality, which for the most part conceals itself behind what he expresses. What he says may often contradict itself; what he lives belongs always to one self-sustaining whole. He has also not sketched his world view in a unified system; he has lived his world view in a unified personality. When we look at his life, then all the contradictions in what he says resolve themselves. They are present in his thinking about the world only in the same sense as in the world itself. He has said this and that about nature. He has never set down his view of nature in a solidly built thought-structure. But when we look over his individual thoughts in this area they, of themselves join together into a whole. One can make a mental picture for oneself of what thought-structure would have arisen if he had presented his views completely and in relationship to each other. I have set myself the task of portraying in this book how Goethe's personality must have been constituted in its innermost being in order for him to be able to express thoughts about the phenomena of nature like the ones he set down in his natural scientific works. I know that, with respect to much of what I will say, Goethean statements can be brought that contradict it. My concern in this book, however, is not to give a history of the evolution of his sayings but rather to present the foundations of his personality that led him to his deep insights into the creating and working of nature. It is not from the numerous statements in which he leans upon other ways of thinking in order to make himself understood, nor in which he makes use of formulations that one or another philosopher had used that these foundations can be known. From what he said to Eckermann one could construct a Goethe for oneself who could never have written *The Metamorphosis of the Plants*. Goethe has addressed many a word to Zelter that could mislead someone to infer a scientific attitude that contradicts his great thoughts about how the animals are formed. I admit that in Goethe's personality forces were at work that I have not considered. But these forces recede before the actually determining ones that give his world view its stamp. To characterize these determining forces as sharply as I possibly can is the task I have set myself. In reading this book one must therefore heed the fact that I nowhere had any intention of allowing parts of any world view of my own to glimmer through my presentation of the Goethean way of picturing things. I believe that in a book of this kind one has no right to put forward one's own world view in terms of *content,* but rather that one has the duty to use what one's own world view gives one for *understanding* what is portrayed. I wanted, for example, to portray Goethe's relationship to the development of Western thought in the way that this relationship presents itself from the point of view of the Goethean world view. For the consideration of the world views of *individual* personalities, this way seems to me to be the only one that guarantees historical objectivity. Another way has to be entered upon only when such a world view is considered in relationship to other ones.

I

Goethe's Place in the Development of Western Thought
Goethe and Schiller

Goethe tells of a conversation that once unfolded between Schiller and himself after both had attended a meeting of the society of natural research in Jena. Schiller was little satisfied with what had been presented in the meeting. A fragmented way of looking at nature had met him there. And he remarked that such a way could not appeal at all to laymen. Goethe replied that it would perhaps remain strange even to the initiated themselves and that there could be yet another way of presenting nature, not as something separated and isolated but rather as working and alive, as striving from the whole into the parts. And now Goethe developed the great ideas that had arisen in him about the nature of the plants. He sketched "with many a characteristic pen-stroke, a symbolic plant" before Schiller's eyes. This symbolic plant was meant to express the being that lives in every individual plant no matter what particular forms the plant might assume. It was meant to show the successive becoming of the individual plant parts, their emerging from each other, and their relatedness to each other. About this symbolic plant shape Goethe, on April 17, 1787 in Palermo, wrote down the words, "There must after all be such a one! How would I otherwise know that this or that formation is a plant, if they were not all formed according to the same model?" Goethe had developed within him the mental picture of a malleable-ideal form that reveals itself to the spirit when it looks out over the manifoldness of plant shapes and is attentive to what they have in common. Schiller contemplated this formation, which supposedly lived not in one single plant but rather in all plants, and said, shaking his head, "That is not an experience; that is an idea." These words appeared to Goethe as though coming from a foreign world. He was conscious of the fact that he had arrived at his symbolic shape through the same kind of naive perception as the mental picture of a thing that one can see with one's eyes and grasp with one's hands. Like the individual plant, the symbolic or archetypal plant was for him an objective being. He believed he had not arbitrary speculation but rather unbiased observation to thank for the archetypal plant. He could not respond with anything other than, "I can be very glad, then, when I have ideas without knowing it, *and in fact even see them with my eyes.*" And he was extremely unhappy as Schiller rejoined with the words, "How can an experience ever be given that could be considered to correspond to an idea. For the characteristic nature of the idea consists in the fact that no experience could ever coincide with it. "

Two opposing world views confront each other in this conversation. Goethe sees in the idea of a thing an element that is immediately present within the thing, working and creating in it. In his view an individual thing takes on particular forms because the idea must, in a given case, live itself out in a specific way. It makes no sense to Goethe to say that a thing does not correspond to the idea. For the thing cannot be anything else than that into which the idea has made it. Schiller thinks otherwise. For him the world of ideas and the world of experience are two separate realms. To experience belong the manifold things and events that fill space and time. Confronting it there stands the realm of ideas as a differently constituted reality of which reason takes possession. Because man's knowledge flows to him from two sides, from without through observation and from within through thinking, Schiller distinguishes two sources of knowledge. For Goethe there is only *one* source of knowledge, the world of experience, in which the world of ideas is included. For him it is impossible to say, "experience *and* idea," because to him the idea lies, through spiritual experience, before the spiritual eye in the same way that the sense world lies before the physical eye.

Schiller's view came from the philosophy of his time. One must seek in Greek antiquity for the underlying mental pictures that have given this philosophy its stamp, and that have become driving forces of our entire Western spiritual development. One can gain a picture of the particular nature of the Goethean world view if one tries in a certain way, with ideas that one borrows solely from it, to characterize this world view entirely out of it itself. This is to be striven for in the later parts of this book. Such a characterization can be aided, however, by taking a preliminary look at the fact that Goethe expressed himself about certain things in one way or another because he felt himself to be in agreement with, or in opposition to, what others thought about some region of natural or spiritual life. Many a statement of Goethe's becomes comprehensible only when one looks at the ways of picturing things that he found confronting him and with which he came to terms in order to gain his own point of view. How he thought and felt about one thing or another gives insight at the same time into the nature of his own world view. If one wants to speak about this region of Goethe's being, one must bring to expression much that for him remained only unconscious feeling. In the conversation with Schiller described here, there stood before Goethe's spiritual eye a world view antithetical to his own. And this antithesis shows how he felt about that way of picturing things which, originating from one aspect of Hellenism, sees an abyss between sense experience and spiritual experience, and how he, without any such abyss, saw the experience of the senses and the experience of the spirit unite in a world picture that communicated reality to him. If one wants to bring to life consciously within oneself as thought what Goethe carried within him more or less unconsciously as his view about the form of Western world views, then these thoughts would be the following ones. In a fateful moment, a mistrust of the human sense organs took possession of a Greek thinker. He began to believe that these organs do not transmit the truth but rather that they deceive him. He lost his trust in what naive, unbiased observation offers. He found that thinking makes different statements about the true being of things than experience does. It would be difficult to say in whose head this mistrust first established itself. One encounters it in the Eleatic school of philosophers whose first representative was Xenophanes, born about 570 B.C. in Kolophon. Parmenides appears as the most important personality of this school, for he has maintained, with a keenness like none before him, that there are two sources of human knowledge. He declared that our sense impressions are delusion and error, and that man can attain knowledge of what is true only through pure thinking that takes no account of experience. Through the way this conception of thinking and of sense experience arose with Parmenides, there was instilled into many following philosophies a developmental illness from which scientific endeavors still suffer today. To discuss the origin in Oriental views of this way of picturing things is out of place within the framework of the Goethean world view.

The Platonic World View

With the admirable boldness characteristic of him, Plato expresses this mistrust of experience: the things of this world, which our senses perceive, have no true being at all; *they are always becoming but never are.* They have only a relative existence. They exist, in their totality, only in and through their relationship to each other; *one can therefore just as well call their whole existence a non-existence.* They are consequently also not objects of any actual knowledge. For, only about what exists, in and for itself and always in the same way, can there be such knowledge; they, on the other hand, are only the object of what we, through sensation, take them to be. As long as we are limited only to our perception of them, we are like people who sit in a dark cave so firmly bound that they cannot even turn their heads and who see nothing except, on the wall facing them, by the light of a fire burning behind them, the *shadow images of real things* that are led across between them and the fire, and who in fact also see of each other, yes each of himself, only *the shadows on that wall. Their wisdom, however, would be to predict the sequence of those shadows that they have learned to know from experience.*

The Platonic view tears the picture of the world-whole into two parts, into the mental picture of a seeming world and into a world of ideas to which alone true eternal reality is thought to correspond. "What alone can be called truly existing, because they always are, but never become nor pass away, are the ideal archetypal images of those shadow images, are the eternal ideas, the archetypal forms of all things. To them no multiplicity can be ascribed; for each is by its very nature only *one,* insofar as it is the archetypal picture itself, whose copies or shadows are all the single transitory things that bear the same name and are of the same kind. To them can also be ascribed no arising and passing away; for they are truly existing, never becoming, however, nor perishing like their copies that vanish away. Of them alone, therefore, is there actual knowledge, since only that can be the object of such knowledge which always and in every respect is, not that which is, but then again is not, depending on how one looks at it. "

The separation of idea and perception is justified only when one speaks of how human knowledge comes about. The human being must allow things to speak to him in a twofold way. They tell him one part of their being of their own free will. He need only listen to them. This is the part of reality that is free of ideas. The other part, however, he must coax from them. He must bring his thinking into movement, and then his inner life fills with the ideas of things. Within the inner life of the personality is the stage upon which things also reveal their ideal inner life. There they speak out what remains eternally hidden to outer perception. The being of nature breaks here into speech. But it is only due to our human organization that things must become known through the sounding together of two tones. In nature *one* stimulator is there that brings forth both tones. The unbiased person listens to their consonance. He recognizes in the ideal language of his own inner life the statements that things allow to come to him. Only someone who has lost his impartiality will interpret the matter differently. He believes that the language of his inner life comes out of a different realm from the language of outer perception. Plato became conscious of what weight the fact has for man's world view that the world reveals itself to the human being from two sides. Out of his insightful valuation of this fact, he recognized that reality cannot be attributed to the sense world, regarded only by itself. Only when the world of ideas lights up out of his soul life, and man, in looking at the world, can place before his spirit idea and sense observation as a unified knowledge experience does he have true reality before him. What sense observation has before itself, without its being shone through by the light of ideas, is a world of semblance. Regarded in this way light is also shed by Plato's insight upon the view of Parmenides as to the deceptive nature of sense-perceptible things. And one can say that the philosophy of Plato is one of the most sublime edifices of thought that has ever sprung from the spirit of mankind. Platonism is the conviction that the goal of all striving for knowledge must be to acquire the *ideas* that carry the world and that constitute its foundation. Whoever cannot awaken this conviction within himself does not understand the Platonic world view. Insofar as Platonism has taken hold in the evolution of Western thought, however, it shows yet another side. Plato did not stop short at emphasizing the knowledge that, in *human perception* the sense world becomes a mere semblance if the light of the world of ideas is not shone upon it, but rather, through the way he presented this fact, he furthered the belief that the sense world, in and for itself, irrespective of man, is a world of semblance, and that true reality is to be found only in ideas. Out of this belief there arises the question: how do idea and sense world (nature) come together outside the human being? For someone who, outside of man, can acknowledge no sense world devoid of ideas, the question about the relationship of idea and sense world is one that must be sought and solved within the being of man. And this is how the matter stands for the Goethean world view. For it, the question, "What relationship exists *outside of man* between idea and sense world?" is an unhealthy one, because for it there is no sense world (nature) without idea *outside of man.* Only man can detach the idea from the sense world for himself and thus *picture* nature to be devoid of idea. Therefore one can say: for the Goethean world view the question, "How do idea and sense-perceptible things come together?" which has occupied the evolution of Western thought for centuries, is an entirely superfluous question. And the results of *this* stream of Platonism, running through the evolution of Western thought, which confronted Goethe, for example, in the above conversation with Schiller, but also in other cases, worked upon his feelings like an unhealthy element in man's way of picturing things. Something he did not express clearly in words but which lived in his feelings and became an impulse that helped shape his own world view is the view that what healthy human feeling teaches us at every moment—namely how the language of observation and that of thinking unite in order to reveal full reality—was not heeded by the thinkers sunk in their reflections. Instead of looking at how nature speaks to man, they fashioned artificial concepts about the relationship of the world of ideas and experience. In order to see the full extent of the deep significance of this direction of thought, which Goethe felt to be unhealthy, within the world views confronting him and by which he wanted to orient himself, one must consider how the stream of Platonism just indicated, which evaporates the sense world into a mere semblance and which thereby brings the world of ideas into a distorted relationship to it, one must consider how this Platonism has grown stronger through a one-sided philosophical apprehension of Christian truth in the course of the evolution of Western thought. Because the Christian view confronted Goethe as connected with the stream of Platonism that he felt to be unhealthy, he could only with difficulty develop a relationship with Christianity. Goethe did not follow in detail how the stream of Platonism that he rejected worked on in the evolution of Christian thought, but he did feel the results of it working on within the ways of thinking that confronted him. Therefore a study of how these results came to be in these ways of thinking that developed through the centuries before Goethe came on the scene will shed light on how *his* way of picturing things took shape. The Christian evolution of thought, in many of its representatives, sought to come to terms with belief in the beyond and with the value that sense existence has in the face of the spiritual world. If one surrendered oneself to the view that the relationship of the sense world to the world of ideas has a significance apart from man, then, with the question arising from this, one came into the view of a divine world order. And the church fathers, to whom this question came, had to form thoughts for themselves as to the role played by the Platonic world of ideas within this divine world order. One not only stood in danger thereby of thinking that what unite in human knowing through direct perception, namely idea and sense world, are separated off by themselves outside of man, but one also stood in danger of separating them from each other, so that ideas, outside of what is given to man as nature, now also lead an existence for themselves within a spirituality separated from nature. If one joined this mental picture, which rested on an untrue view of the world of ideas and of the sense world, with the justified view that the divine can never be present in the human soul in full consciousness, then a total tearing apart of the world of ideas and nature resulted. Then one seeks what always should be sought within the human spirit, outside it, within the created world. The archetypal images of all things begin to be thought of as contained within the divine spirit. The world becomes the imperfect reflection of the perfect world of ideas resting in God. The human soul then, as the result of a one-sided apprehension of Platonism, becomes separated from the relationship of idea and "reality." The soul extends what it justifiably thinks to be its relationship to the divine world order out over the relationship that lives *in it* between the world of ideas and the seeming world of the senses. Augustine comes, through a way of looking at things such as this, to views like the following: "Without wavering we want to believe that the thinking soul is not of the same nature as God, for He allows no community, but that the soul can, however, become enlightened through taking part in the nature of God." In this way, then, when this way of picturing things is one-sidedly overdone, the possibility is taken away from the human soul of experiencing, in its contemplation of nature, also the world of ideas as the essential being of reality. And experiencing the ideas is also interpreted as unchristian. The one-sided view of Platonism is extended over Christianity itself. As a philosophical world view, Platonism stays more in the element of thinking. Religious sentiment immerses thinking into the life of feeling and establishes it in this way within man's nature. Anchored this way within man's soul life, the unhealthy element of one-sided Platonism could gain a deeper significance in the evolution of Western thought than if it had remained mere philosophy. For centuries this development of thought stood before questions like these: how does what man forms as ideas stand with respect to the things of reality? Are the concepts that live in the human soul through the world of ideas only mental pictures, names, that have nothing to do with reality? Are they themselves something real that man receives through perceiving reality and through grasping it with his intellect? For the Goethean world view, such questions are not intellectual questions about something or other lying outside of man's being. Within human contemplation of reality these questions solve themselves with inexhaustible liveliness through true human knowing. And this Goethean world view must not only find that within Christian thoughts there live the results of a one-sided Platonism, but it feels itself estranged from genuine Christianity when the latter confronts him permeated with such Platonism. What lives in many of the thoughts that Goethe developed within himself in order to make the world comprehensible to himself was rejection of that stream of Platonism that he experienced as unhealthy. The fact that besides this he had an open sense for the Platonic lifting of the human soul up to the world of ideas is attested to by many a statement made in this direction. He felt within himself the active working of the reality of ideas when, in his way, he approached nature through contemplation and research; he felt that nature itself spoke in the language of ideas, when the soul opens itself to such language. But he could not agree that one regard the world of ideas as something isolated and thus create for oneself the possibility, with respect to an idea about the nature of plants, of saying: that is no experience, that is an idea. He felt there that his spiritual eye beheld the idea as a reality, just as the physical eye sees the physical part of the plant being. Thus that Platonism which is directed into the world of ideas established itself in all its purity in Goethe's world view, and the stream of Platonism that leads away from reality is overcome in it. Because his world view took this form, Goethe had also to reject what presented itself to him as Christian views in such a way that it could only appear to him to be transformed one-sided Platonism. And he had to feel that in the forms of many a world view which confronted him and with which he wanted to come to terms, one had not succeeded in overcoming within Western culture the Christian-Platonic view of reality that was not in accordance with nature nor with ideas.

The Consequences of the Platonic World View

In vain did Aristotle protest against the Platonic splitting of the world picture. He saw in nature a unified being, that contains ideas just as much as it does the things and phenomena perceptible to the senses. Only within the human spirit can the ideas have an independent existence. But in this independent state they cannot be credited with any reality. Only the soul can separate them from the perceptible things with which, together, they constitute reality. If Western philosophy had linked onto the rightly understood views of Aristotle, then it would have been preserved from much of what must appear to the Goethean world view as aberration.

But Aristotle, rightly understood, to begin with made uncomfortable many a person who wanted to gain a foundation in thought for the Christian picture of things. Many a person who considered himself to be a genuinely "Christian" thinker did not know what to do with a conception of nature that places the highest active principle into the world of our experience. Many Christian philosophers and theologians therefore gave a new interpretation to Aristotle. They attached a meaning to his views which, in their opinion, was able to serve as a logical support for Christian dogma. Man's spirit should not *seek* within things for their creative ideas. The truth is, indeed, imparted to human beings by God in the form of revelation. Reason is only meant to *confirm* what God has revealed. Aristotelian principles were interpreted by the Christian thinkers of the Middle Ages in such a way that the religious truth of salvation received its philosophical reinforcement through these principles. It is the conception of Thomas Aquinas, the most significant Christian thinker, which first seeks to weave the Aristotelian thoughts as far and as deeply into the Christian evolution of ideas as was possible at the time of this thinker. According to this conception, revelation contains the highest truths, the Bible's teachings of salvation; it is possible, however, for reason to penetrate deeply into things, in the Aristotelian way, and to bring forth from them their content of ideas. Revelation can descend far enough, and reason can lift itself high enough, that the teaching of salvation and human knowledge merge with one another at a certain boundary. Aristotle's way of penetrating into things serves Thomas, therefore, as a way of coming to the realm of revelation.

*

When, with Bacon of Verulam and Descartes, an era began in which there asserted itself the will to seek the truth through the human personality's own power, then habits of thought tended to lead one to strive only to set up views which, in spite of their seeming independence from the preceding Western world picture, were nevertheless nothing but new forms of it. Bacon and Descartes had also acquired, as heritage of a degenerate thought world, the pernicious way of looking at the relationship of experience and idea. Bacon had a sense and an understanding only for the particulars of nature. By collecting that which, extending through the manifoldness of space and time, is alike or similar, he believed he arrived at general rules about the processes of nature. Goethe aptly says of him, "For, though he himself always indicates that one should collect the particulars only in order to be able to choose from them, to order them, and finally to arrive at universals, *nevertheless, he grants too many rights to the individual cases,* and before one can achieve through induction—even the induction which he extols—this simplification and conclusion, the life is gone and the forces consume themselves." For Bacon these general rules are a means by which it is possible for reason to have a comfortable overview of the region of particularities. But he does not believe that these rules are founded in the ideal content of things and that they are really creative forces of nature. Therefore he also does not seek the idea directly within the particular but rather abstracts it out of a multiplicity of particulars. Someone who does not believe that the idea lives within the individual thing also can have no inclination to seek it there. He accepts the thing the way it presents itself to mere outer perception. Bacon's significance is to be sought in the fact that he drew attention to that outer way of looking at things which had been denigrated by the one-sided Platonism characterized above, that he emphasized that in it lies a source of truth. He was not, however, in a position to help the world of ideas in the same way to establish its rights over against the perceptible world. He declared what is ideal to be a subjective element within the human spirit. His way of thinking is Platonism in reverse. Plato sees reality only in the world of ideas, Bacon only in the world of perception without ideas. Within Bacon's conception there lies the starting point for that attitude of thinkers by which natural scientists are governed right into the present-day. Bacon's conception suffers from an incorrect view about the ideal element of the world of experience. It could not deal rightly with that medieval view, produced by a one-sided way of posing the question, to the effect that ideas are only names, not realities lying within things.

*

From other points of view, but no less influenced by one-sidedly Platonizing modes of thought, Descartes began his contemplations three decades after Bacon. He is also afflicted with the original sin of Western thought, with mistrust toward the unbiased observation of nature. Doubt in the existence and know ability of things is the starting point of his research. He does not direct his gaze upon the things in order to gain access to certainty, but rather he seeks out a very little door, a way, in the fullest sense of the word, of sneaking in. He withdraws into the most intimate region of thinking. Everything that I have believed up to now as truth might be false, he says to himself. What I have thought might rest upon delusion. But the *one* fact does remain nevertheless: that I think about things. Even if I think lies and illusion, I am thinking nevertheless. And if I think, then I also exist. I think, therefore I am. With this Descartes believes that he has gained a sound starting point for all further thinking about things. He asks himself further: is there not still something else in the content of my thinking that points to a true existence? And there he finds the idea of God as the most perfect of all beings. Given that man himself is imperfect, how does the idea of a most perfect being come into his world of thoughts? An imperfect being cannot possibly produce such an idea out of himself. For the most perfect thing that he can think is in fact an imperfect thing. This idea of the most perfect being must itself therefore have been placed into man. Therefore God must also exist. Why, however, should a perfect being delude us with an illusion? The outer world, which presents itself to us as real, must therefore also be real. Otherwise it would be an illusory picture that the godhead imposes upon us. In this way Descartes seeks to win the trust in reality which, because of inherited feelings, he lacked at first. He seeks truth in an extremely artificial way. He takes his start one-sidedly from thinking. He credits thinking alone with the power to produce conviction. A conviction about observation can only be won if it is provided by thinking. The consequence of this view was that it became the striving of Descartes' successors to determine the whole compass of the truths that thinking can develop out of itself and prove. One wanted to find the sum total of all knowledge out of pure reason. One wanted to take one's start from the simplest immediately clear insights, and proceeding from there to travel through the entire sphere of pure thinking. This system was meant to be built up according to the model of Euclidean geometry. For one was of the view that this also starts from simple, true principles and evolves its entire content through mere deduction, without recourse to observation. In his *Ethics* Spinoza attempted to provide such a system of the pure truths of reason. He takes a number of mental pictures: substance, attribute, mode, thinking, extension, etc., and investigates in a purely intellectual way the relationships and content of these mental pictures. The being of reality supposedly expresses itself in an edifice of thought. Spinoza regards only the knowledge arising through this activity, foreign to reality, as one that corresponds to the true being of the world, as one that provides adequate ideas. The ideas that spring from sense perception are for him inadequate, confused, and mutilated. It is easy to see that also in this world conception there *persists* the one-sided Platonic way of conceiving an antithesis between perceptions and ideas. The thoughts that are formed independently of perception are alone of value for knowledge. Spinoza goes still further. He extends the antithesis also to the moral feeling and actions of human beings. Feelings of pain can only spring from ideas that stem from perception; such ideas produce desires and passions in man, whose slave he can become if he gives himself over to them. Only what springs from reason produces feelings of unqualified pleasure. The highest bliss of man is therefore his life in the ideas of reason, his devotion to knowledge of the pure world of ideas. Whoever has overcome what stems from the world of perception and lives on only within pure knowledge experiences the highest blessedness.

Not quite a century after Spinoza there appears the Scotsman, David Hume, with a way of thinking that again lets knowledge spring from perception alone. Only individual things in space and time are given. Thinking connects the individual perceptions, not, however because something lies within these perceptions themselves that corresponds to this connecting, but rather because the intellect has *habituated* itself to bringing things into relationship. The human being is habituated to seeing that one thing follows another in time. He forms for himself the mental picture that it must follow. He makes the first thing into the cause, the second into the effect. The human being is habituated further to seeing that a movement of his body follows upon a thought of his spirit. He explains this to himself by saying that his spirit has caused the movement of his body. Human ideas are habits of thought, nothing more. Only perceptions have reality.

*

The uniting of the most diverse trends of thought that have come into existence through the centuries is the Kantian world view. Kant also lacks the natural feeling for the relationship between perception and idea. He lives in philosophical preconceptions that he took up into himself through study of his predecessors. One of these preconceptions is that there are necessary truths that are produced by pure thinking free of any experience. The proof of this, in his view, is given by the existence of mathematics and of pure physics which contain such truths. Another of his preconceptions consists of the fact that he denies to experience the ability of attaining equally necessary truths. Mistrust toward the world of perception is also present in Kant. To these habits of thinking there is added the influence of Hume. Kant agrees with Hume with respect to his assertion that the ideas into which thinking combines the individual perceptions do not stem from experience, but rather that thinking adds them to experience. These three preconceptions are the roots of the Kantian thought structure. Man possesses necessary truths. They cannot stem from experience, because it has nothing like them to offer. In spite of this, man applies them to experience. He connects the individual perceptions in accordance with these truths. They stem from man himself. It lies in his nature to bring the things into the kind of relationship that corresponds to the truths gained by pure thinking. Kant goes still further now. He credits the senses also with the ability to bring what is given them from outside into a definite order. This order also does not flow in from outside with the impressions of things. The impressions first receive their order in space and time, through sense perception. Space and time do not belong to the things. The human being is organized in such a way that, when the things make impressions on his senses, he then brings these impressions into spatial or temporal relationships. Man receives from outside only impressions, sensations. The ordering of these in space and in time, the combining of them into ideas, is his own work. But the sensations are also not something that stems from the things. It is not the things that man perceives but only the impressions they make on him. I know nothing about a thing when I have a sensation. I can only say that I notice the arising of a sensation in me. What the characteristics are by which the thing is able to call forth sensations in me, about them I can experience nothing. In Kant's opinion, the human being, does not have to do with the things-in-themselves but only with the impressions that they make upon him and with the relationships into which he himself brings these impressions. The world of experience is not taken up objectively from outside but only, in response to outer causes, subjectively produced from within. It is not the things that give the world of experience the stamp it bears but rather the human organization that does so. That world as such, consequently, is not present at all independently of man. From this standpoint the assumption of necessary truths independent of experience is possible. For these truths relate merely to the way man, of himself, determines his world of experience. They contain the laws of his organization. They have no connection to the things-in-themselves. Kant has therefore found a way out, which permits him to remain in his preconception that there are necessary truths that hold good for the content of the world of experience, without, however, stemming from it. In order to find this way out, he had, to be sure, to commit himself to the view that the human spirit is incapable of knowing anything at all about the things-in-themselves. He had to restrict all knowledge to the world of appearances that the human organization spins out of itself as a result of impressions caused by the things. But why should Kant worry about the being of the things-in-themselves so long as he was able to rescue the eternal, necessarily valid truths in the form in which he pictured them? One-sided Platonism brought forth in Kant a fruit that paralyzes knowledge. Plato turned away from perception and directed his gaze upon the eternal ideas, because perception did not seem to him to express the being of things. Kant, however, renounces the notion that ideas open any real insight into the being of the world, just so they retain the quality of the eternal and necessary. Plato holds to the world of ideas, because he believes that the true being of the world must be eternal, indestructible, unchangeable, and he can ascribe these qualities only to ideas. Kant is content if only he can maintain these qualities for the ideas. Ideas then no longer need to express the being of the world at all.

*

Kant's philosophical way of picturing things was in addition particularly nourished by the direction of his religious feelings. He did not take as his starting point to look, within the being of man, at the living harmony of the world of ideas and of sense perception but rather posed himself the question: through man's experience of the world of ideas, can anything be known by him that can never enter the realm of sense perception? Whoever thinks in the sense of the Goethean world view seeks to know the character of the world of ideas as reality, by grasping the being of the idea through his insight into how the idea allows him to behold reality in the sense-perceptible world of semblance. Then he can ask himself: to what extent, through the character experienced in this way of the world of ideas as reality, can I penetrate into those regions within which the supersensible truths of freedom, of immortality, of the divine world order, find their relationship to human knowledge? Kant negated the possibility of our being able to know anything about the reality of the world of ideas from its relationship to sense perception. From this presupposition he arrived at the scientific result, which, unknown to him, was demanded by the direction of his religious feeling: that scientific knowledge must come to a halt before the kind of questions that relate to freedom, immortality, and the divine world order. There resulted for him the view that human knowledge could only go as far as the boundaries that enclose the sense realm, and that for everything that lies beyond them only faith is possible. He wanted to limit knowing in order to preserve a place for faith. It lies in the sense of the Goethean world view first of all to provide knowing with a firm basis through the fact that the world of ideas, in its essential being, is seen connected with nature, in order then, within the world of ideas thus consolidated, to advance to an experience lying beyond the sense world. Even then, when regions are known that do not lie in the realm of the sense world, one's gaze is still directed toward the living harmony of idea and experience, and certainty of knowledge is sought thereby. Kant could not find any such certainty. Therefore he set out to find, outside of knowledge, a basis for the mental pictures of freedom, immortality, and divine order. It lies in the sense of the Goethean world view to want to know as much about the things-in-themselves as the being of the world of ideas, grasped in connection with nature, allows. It lies in the sense of the Kantian world view to deny to knowledge the right of shining into the world of the things-in-themselves. Goethe wants, within knowledge, to kindle a light that illuminates the being of things. It is also clear to him that the being of the things thus illuminated does not lie within the light itself; but he nevertheless does not want to give up having this being become revealed through the illumination by this light. Kant holds fast to the view that the being of the things illuminated does not lie in the light itself; therefore the light can reveal nothing about this being.

    The world view of Kant can stand before that of Goethe only in the sense of the following mental pictures: Kant's world view has not arisen through any clearing away of old errors, nor through any free, original descending into the depths of reality but rather through a fusing together of acquired and inherited philosophical and religious preconceptions. This world view could only spring from an individual in whom the sense for the living creativity within nature has remained undeveloped. And it could only affect the kind of individuals who suffered from the same lack. From the far-reaching influence that Kant's way of thinking exercised upon his contemporaries, one can see how strongly they stood under the spell of one-sided Platonism.

Goethe and the Platonic World View

I have described the development of thought from Plato's time to Kant's in order to be able to show what impressions Goethe had to receive when he turned to the results of the philosophical thoughts to which he had recourse in order to satisfy his powerful need for knowledge. For the innumerable questions to which his nature urged him, he found no answers in the philosophies. In fact, every time he delved into the world view of some philosopher, an antithesis manifested itself between the direction his questions took and the thought world from which he sought counsel. The reason for this lies in the fact that the one-sided Platonic separation of idea and experience was repugnant to his nature. When he observed nature, it then brought ideas to meet him. He therefore could only think it to be filled with ideas. A world of ideas, which does not permeate the things of nature, which does not bring forth their appearing and disappearing, their becoming and growing, is for him a powerless web of thoughts. The logical spinning out of lines of thought, without descending into the real life and creative activity of nature seems to him unfruitful. For he feels himself intimately intertwined with nature. He regards himself as a living part of nature. What arises within his spirit, according to his view, nature has allowed to arise within him. Man should. not place himself in some corner and believe that he could there spin out of himself a web of thoughts which explains the being of things. He should continuously let the stream of world happening flow through himself. There he will feel that the world of ideas is nothing other than the creative and active power of nature. He will not want to stand above the things in order to think about them, but rather he will delve into their depths and raise out of them what lives and works within them. Goethe's artistic nature led him to this way of thinking. He felt his poetic creations grow forth out of his personality with the same necessity with which a flower blossoms. The way the spirit brought forth a work of art in him seemed to him to be no different than the way nature produces its creations. And as in the work of art the spiritual element is inseparable from its spiritless material, so also it was impossible for him, with a thing of nature, to picture the perception without the idea. A view therefore seemed foreign to him that saw in a perception only something unclear, confused, and which wanted to regard the world of ideas as separate and cleansed of all experience. He felt, in every world view in which the elements of one-sidedly understood Platonism lived, something contrary to nature. Therefore he could not find in the philosophers what he sought from them. He sought the ideas that live in the things and that let all the single things of experience appear as though growing forth out of a living whole, and the philosophers provided him with thought hulls that they had tied together into systems according to logical principles. Again and again he found himself thrown back upon himself when he sought from others the explanations to the riddles with which nature presented him.

Among the things that caused Goethe suffering before his Italian journey was the fact that his need for knowledge could find no satisfaction. In Italy he was able to form a view for himself about the driving forces out of which works of art come. He recognized that in perfect works of art is contained that which human beings revere as something divine, as something eternal. After looking at artistic creations that particularly interest him, he writes the words, "The great works of art have at the same time been brought forth by human beings according to *true* and *natural* laws, as the greatest works of nature. Everything that is arbitrary, thought up, falls away; *there is necessity, there is God.*" The art of the Greeks drew forth this statement from him: "I suspect that the Greeks proceeded according to precisely those laws by which nature itself proceeds and whose tracks I am pursuing." What Plato believed he found in the world of ideas, what the philosophers were never able to bring home to Goethe, this looked out at him from the works of art of Italy. In art there reveals itself to Goethe for the first time in a perfect form what he can regard as the basis of knowledge. He sees in artistic production one kind, and a higher level, of the working of nature; artistic creating is for him a heightened creating of nature. He later expressed this in his characterization of Winckelmann: "...inasmuch as man is placed at the pinnacle of nature, he then regards himself again as an entire nature, which yet again has to bring forth within itself a pinnacle. To this end he enhances himself, by imbuing himself with every perfection and virtue, summons choice, order, harmony, and meaning, *and finally lifts himself to the production of works of art.*" Goethe attains his world view not on a path of logical deduction but rather through contemplation of the being of art. And what he found in art, this he seeks also in nature.

The activity by which Goethe takes possession of a knowledge about something in nature is not essentially different from artistic activity. Both merge into one another and extend over one another. In Goethe's view, the artist must become greater and more decisive when, in addition to having "talent he is a trained botanist as well, when, starting with the roots, he knows what influence the various parts have upon the growth and development of the plant, what they do and how they mutually affect each other, when he has insight into, and reflects upon, the successive development of flowers, leaves, pollination, fruit, and new seed. He will thereupon not merely reveal, through what he selects from the phenomena, his own tastes, but rather, through a correct presentation of individual characteristics, he will also make us feel wonder and teach us at the same time." According to this, a work of art is all the more perfect the more there comes to expression in it the same lawfulness that is contained in the work of nature to which it corresponds. There is only one unified realm of truth, and this comprises art and nature. Therefore the capacity for artistic creativity can also not be essentially different from the capacity to know nature. Goethe says about the style of the artist that it "rests upon the deepest foundations of *knowledge,* upon the being of things, insofar as we are permitted to know it in forms we can see and grasp." The way of looking at things that comes from Platonic conceptions taken up in a one-sided way draws a sharp line between science and art. It lets artistic activity rest upon fantasy, upon feeling. Scientific findings should be the result of the development of concepts free of any fantasy. Goethe pictures the matter differently. When he turns his eye upon nature, there results for him a number of ideas; but he finds that, within the individual object of experience, its ideal component is not closed off; the idea points beyond the individual object to related objects, in which it comes to manifestation in a similar way. The philosophizing observer holds fast to this ideal component and brings it to expression directly in his thought creations. This ideal element also works upon the artist. But it moves him to shape a work, in which the idea does not merely work as it does within a work of nature but rather *comes to direct manifestation.* That which, in the work of nature, is merely ideal and reveals itself to the spiritual eye of the observer, becomes real in the work of art, it becomes perceptible reality. The artist realizes the ideas of nature. But he does not need to bring these to consciousness for himself in the form of ideas. When he contemplates a thing or an event, there then takes shape immediately within his spirit something else, which contains in real manifestation what the thing or event contains only as idea. The artist gives us pictures of the works of nature that transform the idea content of these works into a content of perception. The philosopher shows how nature presents itself to thinking contemplation; the artist shows how nature would look if it openly brought the forces working in it not merely to meet thinking but also to meet perception. It is one and the same truth that the philosopher presents in the form of thought, the artist in the form of a picture. The two differ only in their means of expression. The insight into the true relationship of idea and experience that Goethe acquired in Italy is only the fruit from the seed that lay hidden in his natural predisposition. His Italian journey brought him that warmth of sun which was able to bring the seed to maturity. In the essay "Nature," which in 1782 appeared in the *Tiefurt Journal*, and whose author was Goethe (see my indication of Goethe's authorship in Volume seven of the publications of the Goethe Society), there are already to be found the seeds of the later Goethean world view. What is here dim feeling later becomes clear definite thought. "Nature! We are surrounded and embraced by her, unable to take ourselves out of her, and unable to enter more deeply into her. She takes us up, unasked and unwarned, into the orbit of her dance and drives herself on with us, until we are exhausted and fall from her arms ... she (nature) has *thought* and *muses* continuously; but not as a human being, rather as nature ... She has no language nor speech, but *she creates tongues and hearts, through which she feels and speaks...* I did not speak of her. No, what is true and false, everything, she has spoken. Everything is her fault, everything is to her credit!" As Goethe wrote down these sentences, it was still not yet clear to him how nature expresses her ideal being through man; but he did feel that it is the voice of the spirit of nature that sounds in the spirit of man.

*

In Italy, Goethe found the spiritual atmosphere in which his organs of knowledge could develop themselves, as they, in accordance with their predisposition, would have to if he were to become fully satisfied. In Rome he "discussed art and its theoretical demands a great deal with Moritz." As he traveled and observed the metamorphosis of plants, a method, in accordance with nature, took shape within him that later proved itself to be fruitful for gaining knowledge of all organic nature. "For as the vegetation presented its behavior to me step by step, I could not go wrong, but, while letting it be, I had to recognize the ways and means by which it can gradually help even the most hidden condition to develop to perfection." Only a few years after his return from Italy he succeeded in finding a way of looking at inorganic nature also, born of his spiritual needs. "During physical research the conviction forced itself on me that, in any contemplation of objects, our highest duty is to search out exactly every determining factor under which a phenomenon appears and to aim for the greatest possible completeness of phenomena, because the phenomena are ultimately constrained to connect themselves to each other, or rather to reach over into each other, and they do form, as the researcher looks at them, a kind of organization; they must manifest their whole inner life."

Goethe did not find enlightenment anywhere. He had to enlighten himself. He sought the reason for this and believed to have found it in his lack of an organ for philosophy in the real sense. The reason, however, is to be sought in the fact that the Platonic way of thinking, grasped one-sidedly, which held sway in all the philosophies accessible to him, was contrary to his healthy natural disposition. In his youth he had repeatedly turned to Spinoza. He admits, in fact, that this philosopher had always had a "peaceful effect" upon him. This is based on the fact that Spinoza regards the universe as a great unity and thinks of everything individual as going forth necessarily out of the whole. But when Goethe let himself into the content of Spinoza's philosophy, he felt nevertheless that this content remained alien to him. "But do not think that I would have liked to subscribe to his writings and profess them literally. For, I had already all too clearly recognized that no one understands another, that no one, in relation to the same words, thinks the same thing that another does, that a conversation or a reading stimulate different trains of thought in different people; and one will certainly trust the author of *Werther* and *Faust,* deeply aware as he is of such misunderstandings, not to harbor the presumption of perfectly understanding a man who, as a student of Descartes, has raised himself through mathematical and rabbinical training to the pinnacle of thinking; who, right up to the present day, still seems to be the goal of all speculative efforts." But for Goethe, what made him a philosopher to whom he still could not surrender himself completely was not the fact that Spinoza was schooled by Descartes, and also not the fact that he had raised himself through mathematical and rabbinical training to the pinnacle of thinking but rather his purely logical way, estranged from reality, of dealing with knowledge. Goethe could not surrender to pure thinking free of experience, because he was not able to separate it from the totality of what is real. He did not want, merely logically, to join one thought onto another. Rather, such an activity of thought seemed to him to lead away from true reality. He had to immerse his spirit into experience in order to come to the idea. The reciprocal working of idea and perception was for him a spiritual breathing. "Time is ruled by swings of the pendulum, the moral and scientific world by the reciprocal movement of idea and experience." To regard the world and its phenomena in the sense of this statement seemed natural to Goethe, because for him there was no doubt about the fact that nature follows the same procedure: that it "is a development from a living mysterious whole" to the manifold particular phenomena which fill space and time. The mysterious whole is the world of the idea. "The idea is eternal and single; that we also use the plural is not appropriate. Everything of which we become aware and about which we are able to speak is only a manifestation of the idea; concepts are what we speak, and to this extent the idea itself is a concept." Nature's creating goes from the whole, which is ideal in character, into the particular given to perception as something real. Therefore the observer should "recognize what is ideal within the real and allay his momentary discontent with what is finite by raising himself to the infinite." Goethe is convinced that "nature proceeds according to ideas in the same way that man, in everything he undertakes, pursues an idea." When a person really succeeds in raising himself to the idea and, taking his start from the idea, succeeds in grasping the particulars of perception, he then accomplishes the same thing that nature does when it lets its creations go forth out of the mysterious whole. As long as a person does not feel the working and creating of the idea, his thinking remains separated from living nature. He must then regard his thinking as a merely subjective activity, which can sketch an abstract picture of nature. As soon as he feels, however, how the idea lives and is active within his inner life, he looks upon himself and nature as *one* whole, and what appears as something subjective in his inner life has objective validity for him as well; he knows that he no longer confronts nature as a stranger but rather feels himself grown together with the whole of it. The subjective has become objective; the objective has become entirely permeated with spirit. Goethe is of the opinion that Kant's basic error consists of the fact that he "regards the subjective ability to know as an object itself and, sharply indeed but not entirely correctly, he distinguishes the point where subjective and objective meet." The ability to know appears subjective to a person only so long as he does not heed the fact that it is nature itself that speaks through this ability. Subjective and objective meet when the objective world of ideas arises within the subject and when there lives in the spirit of man that which is active in nature itself. When that is the case, then all antithesis between subjective and objective ceases. This antithesis has significance only so long as a person maintains it artificially, only so long as he regards ideas as *his* thoughts, through which the being of nature is mirrored, but in which this being itself is not at work. Kant and the Kantians had no inkling of the fact that, in the ideas of our reason the being, the "in-itself" of things is experienced directly. For them everything of an ideal nature is merely something subjective. They therefore came to the opinion that what is ideal could be necessarily valid only when that to which it relates, the world of experience, is also only subjective. The Kantian way of thinking stands in sharp opposition to Goethe's views. There are, it is true, isolated statements of Goethe's in which he speaks approvingly of Kant's views. He tells of having been present at many conversations on these views. "With a certain amount of attentiveness I was able to notice that the old cardinal question was being revived as to how much our self and how much the outer world contributes to our spiritual existence. *I had never separated the two,* and when, in my way, I philosophized about things, I did so with unconscious naivety and really believed that I saw my conclusions before my very eyes. But as soon as that dispute arose in the discussion, I liked to range myself on the side that does man the most honor, and fully applauded all the friends who maintained, with Kant, that even though all our knowledge begins with experience, still it does not for that reason all spring from experience." In Goethe's view the idea also does not stem from that part of experience which presents itself to mere perception through the senses of man. Reason, fantasy, must be active, must penetrate into the inner life of beings in order to take possession of the ideal elements of existence. To that extent the spirit of man partakes in the coming about of knowledge. Goethe believes it does man honor that within his spirit the higher reality that is not accessible to his senses comes to manifestation; Kant, on the other hand, denies the world of experience any character of higher reality, because it contains parts which stem from our spirit. Only when he first reinterpreted Kant's principles in the light of his world view could Goethe relate himself favorably to them. The basic elements of Kant's way of thinking are in sharpest opposition to Goethe's nature. If he did not emphasize this opposition sharply enough, that is certainly only due to the fact that he did not involve himself with these basic elements because they were too alien to him. "It was the opening part (of *The Critique of Pure Reason)* that appealed to me; I dared not venture into the labyrinth itself. Sometimes my poetic gift hindered me, sometimes my common sense, and nowhere did I feel myself changed for the better." About his conversations with the Kantians Goethe had to confess, "They certainly heard me but had no answer for me nor could be in any way helpful. It happened to me more than once that one or another of them, with smiling wonderment, admitted that what I said was analogous to the Kantian way of picturing things, but strange." It was, as I have shown, in fact not analogous but rather most emphatically opposite to the Kantian way of picturing things.

*

It is interesting to see how Schiller seeks to shed light for himself upon the antithesis between the Goethean way of thinking and his own. He feels what is original and free in the Goethean world view, but he cannot rid his own spirit of its one-sidedly grasped Platonic elements of thought. He cannot raise himself to the insight that idea and perception are not present within reality in a state of separation from each other but rather are only artificially *thought* to be separated by an intellect that has been led astray by ideas steered in a false direction. Therefore in contrast to the Goethean way of thinking, which Schiller calls an intuitive one, he sets up his own way, as a speculative one, and declares that both ways, if they only work strongly enough, must lead to one and the same goal. Schiller supposes of the intuitive spirit that he holds to the empirical, to the individual, and from there ascends to the law, to the idea. In the case where such a spirit is a genius, he will recognize what is necessary within the empirical, the species within the individual. The speculative spirit, on the other hand, supposedly goes in the opposite direction. The law, the idea, is supposedly given to him first, and from it he descends to the empirical and the individual. If such a spirit is a genius, then he will, in fact, always have only species in view, but with the possibility of life and with a well-founded connection to real objects. The supposition that there is a particular way of thinking, the speculative in contrast to the intuitive, rests upon the belief that the world of ideas is thought to have an isolated existence separate from the world of perception. Were this the case, then there could be a way for the content of ideas about perceptible things to come into the spirit, even if the spirit did not seek it within experience. If, however, the world of ideas is inseparably bound up with the reality of experience, if both are present only as *one* whole, then there can only be an intuitive knowledge that seeks the idea within experience and that also grasps the species along with the individual. In truth there is also no purely speculative spirit in Schiller's sense. For the species exist only within the sphere to which the individuals also belong; and the spirit absolutely cannot find them anywhere else. If a so-called speculative spirit really has ideas of species, then these stem from observation of the real world. If one's living feeling for this origin, for the necessary connection of species with the individual is lost, then there arises the opinion that such ideas can arise in our reason even without experience. The adherents of this opinion label a number of abstract ideas of species as content of pure reason because they do not see the threads by which these ideas are bound to experience. Such a delusion is most easily possible with respect to the most general, most comprehensive ideas. Since such ideas encompass wide areas of reality, much in them is eradicated or dimmed that is attributable to the individuals belonging to this or that area. A number of such general ideas can be taken up from other people and then believed to be innate in man or to be spun out of pure reason. An individual succumbing to such a belief may consider himself to be speculative. But he will never be able to draw from his world of ideas anything more than what those people have put there, from whom he has received these ideas. When Schiller maintains that the speculative spirit, if he is a genius, always creates "only species, but with the possibility of life and with a well-founded connection to real objects" (see Schiller's letter to Goethe of August 23, 1794), he is in error. A really speculative spirit, who lived only in concepts of species, could not find in his world of ideas any well-founded connection to reality other than the one that already lies within it. A spirit who has connections to the reality of nature and who in spite of this calls himself speculative, is caught up in a delusion about his own being. This delusion can mislead him into neglecting his connections with reality, with his immediate life. He will believe himself able to dispense with immediate observation, because he believes himself to have other sources of truth. The result of this is always that the world of ideas of such a spirit has a dull and faded character. The fresh colors of life will be lacking in his thoughts. Whoever wants to live in association with reality will not be able to gain much from such a world of thoughts. The speculative way cannot be regarded as a way of thinking that can stand with equal validity beside the intuitive one but rather as an atrophied way of thinking, impoverished of life. The intuitive spirit does not have to do merely with individuals; he does not *seek* within the empirical for the character of necessity. But rather, when he turns to nature, perception and idea join themselves together directly into a unity for him. Both are seen as existing within one another and are felt to be a whole. While he can ascend to the most general truths, to the loftiest abstractions, immediate real life will always be recognizable in his world of thoughts. Goethe's thinking was of this kind. Heinroth made an apt statement in his anthropology about this thinking that pleased Goethe mightily, because it gave him insight into his own nature. "Dr. Heinroth ... speaks favorably about my being and working; he even describes my way of going about things as an original one: that my ability to think, namely, is active *objectively,* by which he means that my thinking does not separate itself from the objects; that the elements of the objects, one's perceptions, go into thinking and become most inwardly permeated by it; that my perceiving is itself a thinking, my thinking a perceiving." Basically Heinroth is describing nothing other than the way any healthy thinking relates itself to objects. Any other way of going about things is an aberration from the natural way. If perception predominates in a person, then he gets stuck at what is individual; he cannot penetrate into the deeper foundations of reality; if abstract thinking predominates in him, then his concepts seem insufficient to understand the living fullness of what is real. The raw empiricist, who contents himself with the individual facts, represents the extreme of the first aberration; the other extreme is given in the philosopher who worships pure reason and who only thinks, without having any feeling for the fact that thoughts, by their very nature, are bound to perception. Goethe describes, in a beautiful picture, the feeling of the thinker who ascends to the highest truths without losing his feeling for living experience. At the beginning of 1784 he writes an essay on granite. He goes out upon a mountaintop of this stone, where he can say to himself, "You rest here directly upon a ground that reaches into the deepest places of the earth; no newer layers, no ruins, heaped or swept together, have laid themselves between you and the solid ground of the primeval world; you do not walk here, as in those fruitful valleys, upon a continuous grave; these peaks have brought forth no living thing and have devoured no living thing; they are before all life and above all life. In this moment, when the inner attracting and moving powers of the earth are working as though directly upon me, when the influences of the heavens are hovering around me more closely, I become attuned to higher contemplations of nature, and just as the human spirit enlivens all, so there stirs in me also a parable, whose sublimity I cannot withstand. So lonely, I say to myself as I look down this completely bare peak and scarcely make out in the distance at the foot a meager moss growing, so lonely, I say, does the mood of a man become, who wants to open his soul *only to the oldest, first, and deepest feelings of truth.* Yes, he can say to himself: here, upon the most ancient, eternal altar, which is built directly upon the deeps of creation, I bring an offering to the being of all beings. I feel the primal and most solid beginnings of our existence; I look out over the world, upon its more rugged and more gentle valleys and upon its distant fruitful meadows; my soul rises above itself and above all, and longs for the heavens nearer it. But soon the burning sun calls back thirst and hunger, his human needs. *He looks back upon those valleys* from which his spirit had already soared." Only that person can develop within himself such an enthusiasm of knowledge, such feelings for the oldest sound truths, who again and again finds his way out of the regions of the world of ideas back into direct perceptions.

Personality and World View

Man learns to know the outer side of nature through perception; its deeper-lying driving powers reveal themselves within his own inner life as subjective experiences. In philosophical contemplation of the world and in artistic feeling and creating, his subjective experiences permeate his objective perceptions. What had to split itself into two parts in order to penetrate into the human spirit becomes again one whole. The human being satisfies his highest spiritual needs when he incorporates into the objectively perceived world what the world manifests to him within his inner life as its deeper mysteries. Knowledge and artistic creations are nothing other than perceptions filled with man's inner experiences. In the simplest judgment about a thing or event of the outer world, there can be found a human soul experience and an outer perception in inner association with one another. When I say that one body strikes another, I have already brought an inner experience into the outer world. I see a body in motion; it hits another one; this one also comes into motion as a consequence. The content of the perception cannot tell me more than this. I am not satisfied by this, however. For I feel that still more is present in the whole phenomenon than what mere perception gives me. I reach for an inner experience that will enlighten me about the perception. I know that I myself can set a body into motion by applying force, by striking it. I carry this experience over into the phenomenon and say that the one body strikes the other. "The human being never realizes just how anthropomorphic he is" (Goethe, *Aphorisms in Prose,* Kuerschner edition, Vol. 36, 2, p. 353). There are people who, from the presence of this subjective component in every judgment about the outer world, draw the conclusion that reality's objective core of being is inaccessible to man. They believe that man falsifies the immediate and objective factual state of reality when he lays his subjective experiences into reality. They say that because man can picture the world to himself only through the lens of his subjective life, all his knowledge is only a subjective, limitedly human one. Someone, however, who comes to consciousness about what manifests itself within the inner life of man will want to have nothing to do with such unfruitful assertions. He knows that truth comes about precisely through the fact that perception and idea permeate each other in the human process of knowledge. It is clear to him that in the subjective there lives what is most archetypically and most profoundly objective. "When the healthy nature of man works as a whole, when he feels himself in the world as though in a great, beautiful, worthy, and precious whole, when his harmonious sense of well-being imparts to him a pure free delight, *then the universe, if it could experience itself, would, as having achieved its goal, exult with joy and marvel at the pinnacle of its own becoming and being.*" The reality accessible to mere perception is only one half of complete reality; the content of the human spirit is the other half. If no human being ever confronted the world, then this second half would never come to living manifestation, to full existence. It would work, it is true, as a hidden world of forces; but the possibility would be taken from it of revealing itself in its own form. One could say that, without man, the world would reveal an untrue countenance. The world would be as it is, through its deeper forces, but these deeper forces would themselves remain cloaked by what they bring about. Within man's spirit they are delivered from their enchantment. Man is not there in order merely to make a picture for himself of a completed world; no, he himself works along with the coming into being of this world.

*

The subjective experiences of different people take different forms. For those who do not believe in the objective nature of the inner world, that is one more reason to deny man the ability to penetrate into the being of things. For how can something be the being of things which appears to one person one way and to another person another way. For the person who recognizes the true nature of the inner world, there follows from the differences of inner experiences only that nature can express its rich content in different ways. The truth appears to each individual person in an individual garb. It adapts itself to the particularities of his personality. This is especially the case with the highest truths that are most important to man. In order to attain them, man carries over into the perceptible world his most intimate spiritual experiences, and along with them what is most individual in his personality. There are also generally accepted truths that every human being takes up without giving them an individual coloring. These are, however, the most superficial and trivial ones. They correspond to the general characteristics of man as a species that are the same for everyone. Certain qualities that are the same in all human beings also produce the same judgments about things. The way people regard things according to measurement and number is the same for everyone. Therefore everyone finds the same mathematical truths. But within the particular qualities by which the individual personality lifts himself from the general characteristics of his species, there also lies the basis for the individual forms that he gives to truth. The point is not whether the truth appears differently in one person than in another but rather whether all the individual forms coming into view belong to one single whole, to the one unified ideal world. The truth speaks different languages and dialects within the inner life of individual people; in every great human being it speaks an individual language that belongs only to this one personality. But it is always one truth that speaks there. "If I know my relationship to myself and to the outer world, then I call it truth. And in this way each person can have his own truth, and it is after all always the same one." This is Goethe's view. The truth is not some petrified, dead system of concepts, capable of assuming only one form; it is a living sea, within which the spirit of man lives, and which can show on its surface waves of the most varied form. "Theory, in and for itself, is of no use, but only inasmuch as it makes us believe in the connections of phenomena," says Goethe. He values no theory that claims completeness once and for all and is supposed to represent in this form an eternal truth. He wants living concepts by which the spirit of the individual person, according to his individual nature, draws his perceptions together. *To know* the truth means for him *to live in the truth.* And to live in the truth is nothing other than, when looking at each individual thing, to watch what inner experience occurs when one stands in front of this thing. Such a view of human knowledge cannot speak of limits of knowing, nor of a restriction of knowing imposed by man's nature. For the questions that knowledge, according to this view, poses itself do not spring from the things; they are also not imposed upon man by *any* other power lying outside of his personality. They spring from the nature of his personality itself. When man directs his gaze upon a thing, there then arises in him the urge to see more than what approaches him in his perception. And as far as this urge reaches, so far does his need for knowledge also reach. Where does this urge originate? Actually only from the fact that an inner experience feels itself stimulated within the soul to enter into a connection with the perception. As soon as the connection is accomplished, the need for knowledge is also satisfied. Wanting to know is a demand of human nature and not of the things. These can tell man no more about their being than he demands from them. Someone who speaks of a limitation of knowledge's capabilities does not know where the need for knowledge originates. He believes that the content of truth lies stored up somewhere, and that in man there lives only the indistinct wish to find access to the place where it is stored. But it is the very being of the things that works itself out of the inner life of man and strives to where it belongs: to the perception. It is not after something hidden that man strives in the knowledge process but rather after the balancing out of two forces that work upon him from two sides. One can well say that without man there would be no knowledge of the inner life of things, for without him there would be nothing there through which this inner life could express itself. But one cannot say that there is something in the inner life of things that is inaccessible to man. The fact that something else is present in things than what perception gives him, this man knows only because this something else lives within his own inner life. To speak of a further unknown something in things means to make up words about something that is not present.

*

Those who are not able to recognize that it is the language of the things that is spoken in the inner life of man are of the view that all truth must penetrate into man from outside. Such persons hold fast either to mere perception and believe they can know the truth only through seeing, hearing, touching, through gathering together historical events, and through comparing, counting, calculating, weighing what is taken up out of the world of facts; or they are of the view that the truth can come to man only when it is revealed to him in a way set apart from knowledge; or, finally, they want through forces of a particular kind, through ecstasy or mystical vision, to come into possession of the highest insights which, in their view, the world of ideas accessible to thinking cannot offer them. In addition, metaphysicians of a particular sort connect themselves to those who think in the Kantian sense and to the one-sided mystics. To be sure, these seek through thinking to form concepts of the truth for themselves. But they seek the content for these concepts not in the human world of ideas but rather in a second reality lying behind the things. They believe themselves able, through pure concepts, either to determine something certain about a content of this kind or, at least, through hypotheses, to be able to form mental pictures of it. I am speaking here, to begin with, about the kind of people mentioned first, the fact fanatics. Every now and then they become conscious of the fact that, in counting and calculating, there already takes place with the help of thinking a working through of the content of perception. Then, however, they say that this thought work is merely the *means* by which man struggles to know the relationship of the facts. What flows from thinking in the act of working upon the outer world represents to them something merely subjective; they consider to be the objective content of truth, the valid content of knowledge, only what approaches them from outside with the help of thinking. They catch the facts, to be sure, in the net of their thoughts but allow objective validity only to what is caught. They overlook the fact that what is thus caught by thinking undergoes an exposition, an ordering, an interpretation, which it does not have in mere perception. Mathematics is a result of pure thought processes; its content is a spiritual, subjective one. And the mechanic, who pictures the processes of nature in mathematical relationships, can do this only under the presupposition that these relationships are founded in the nature of these processes. But this means nothing other than that within perception a mathematical order is hidden which only that person sees who has developed the mathematical laws within his spirit. Between the mathematical and mechanical perceptions and the most intimate spiritual experiences, however, there is no difference in kind but only in degree. And man can carry other inner experiences, other areas of his world of ideas over into his perceptions with the same justification as he does the results of mathematical research. The fact fanatic only *seems* to ascertain purely outer processes. He usually does not reflect upon his world of ideas and its character as subjective experience. His inner experiences are also bloodless abstractions, poor in content, that are obscured by the powerful content of facts. The illusion to which he surrenders himself can last only as long as he remains at the lowest level of interpreting nature, as long as he merely counts, weighs, and calculates. At the higher levels the true nature of knowledge is soon borne in upon him. But one can observe about the fact fanatics that they stick primarily to the lower levels. They are therefore like an aesthetician who wants to judge a piece of music only by what can be calculated and counted in it. They want to separate the phenomena of nature from man. Nothing subjective must flow into observation. Goethe condemns this approach with the words, "Man in himself, insofar as he uses his healthy senses, is the greatest and most accurate physical apparatus that there can be, and that is precisely what is of the greatest harm to modern physics, that one has, as it were, separated experiments from man and wants to know nature merely through what manmade instruments show, yes wants to limit and prove thereby what nature can do." It is fear of the subjective that leads to such a way of doing things and that comes from a misapprehension of the true nature of the subjective. "But man stands so high precisely through the fact that what otherwise could not manifest itself does manifest itself in him. For what is a string and all its mechanical divisions compared to the ear of the musician? Yes, one can say, what are the elemental phenomena of nature themselves compared to man who must first tame and modify them all in order to be able to assimilate them to some extent?" In Goethe's view the natural scientist should be attentive not only to how things appear but rather to how they would appear if everything that works in them as ideal driving forces were also actually to come to outer manifestation. Only when the bodily and spiritual organism of man places itself before the phenomena do they then reveal their inner being.

Whoever approaches the phenomena in a spirit of observing them freely and openly, and with a developed inner life in which the ideas of things manifest themselves, to him the phenomena—it is Goethe's view—reveal everything about themselves. There stands in opposition to Goethe's world view, therefore, the one that does not seek the being of things within experienceable reality but rather within a second reality lying behind this one. In Fr. H. Jacobi, Goethe encountered an adherent of such a world view. Goethe gives vent to his displeasure in a remark in the *Tag- und Jahresheft* (1811): "Jacobi's *Of Divine Things* made me unhappy. How could the book of such a beloved friend be welcome to me when I had to see developed in it the thesis that nature conceals God. With my pure, deep, inborn, and trained way of looking at things, which had taught me absolutely to see God in nature, nature in God, such that this way of picturing things constituted the foundation of my whole existence, would not such a peculiar, one-sidedly limited statement estrange me forever in spirit from this most noble man whose heart I revered and loved?" Goethe's way of looking at things gives him the certainty that he experiences an eternal lawfulness in his permeation of nature with ideas, and this eternal lawfulness is for him identical with the divine. If the divine did conceal itself behind the things of nature and yet constituted the creative element in them, it could not then be *seen;* man would have to *believe* in it. In a letter to Jacobi, Goethe defends his *seeing* in contrast to *faith:* "*God has punished you with metaphysics* and set a thorn in your flesh but has blessed *me* with *physics.* I will stick to the reverence for God of the atheist (Spinoza) and *leave to you* everything you call, and would like to call, religion. You are for *faith* in God; I am for *seeing.*" Where this seeing ends, the human spirit then has nothing to seek. We read in his *Aphorisms in Prose:* "Man is really set into the midst of a real world and endowed with such organs that he can know and bring forth what is real and what is possible along with it. All healthy people are convinced of their existence and of something existing around them. For all that, there is *a hollow spot in the brain,* which means a place where no object is mirrored, just as in the eye itself there is a little spot that does not see. If a person becomes particularly attentive to this place, becomes absorbed with it, he then succumbs to an *illness of the spirit,* has inklings here of *things of another world,* which, however, *are actually non-things* and have neither shape nor limitations but rather, as *empty night-spaces,* cause fear and pursue in a more than ghost-like way the person who does not tear himself free." Out of this same mood there is the aphorism, "The highest would be to grasp that everything facual is already theory. The blue of the heavens reveals to us the basic law of the science of colors. *Only do not seek anything behind the phenomena; they are themselves the teachings.*"

Kant denies to man the ability to penetrate into the region of nature in which its creative forces *become* directly *visible.* In his opinion concepts are abstract units into which the human intellect draws together the manifold particulars of nature but which have nothing to do with the *living* unity, with the creative wholeness of nature from which these particulars really proceed. The human being experiences in this drawing together only a subjective operation. He can relate his general concepts to his empirical perception; but these concepts in themselves are not alive, productive, in such a way that man could see what is individual proceed out of them. For Kant concepts are dead units present only in man. "Our intellect is a capacity for concepts, i.e., it is a discursive intellect, for which, to be sure, it must be a matter of chance what and how different the particular thing might be which is given to it in nature and what can be brought under its concepts." This is how Kant characterizes the intellect (Paragraph 77 of *Critique of Judgment).* The following necessarily results from this: "It is a matter of infinite concern to our reason not to let go of the mechanism of nature in its creations and not to pass it by in explaining them, because without this mechanism no insight into the nature of things can be attained. If one right away concedes to us that a supreme architect has directly created the forms of nature just as they have been from the very beginning, or has predetermined them in such a way that they, in nature's course, continually shape themselves upon the very same model, then even so our knowledge of nature has not thereby been furthered in the least; *because we do not at all know that architect's way of doing things, nor his ideas* which supposedly contain the principles of the possibilities of the beings of nature, and we are not able by him to explain nature from above downward, as it were *(a priori)"* (Paragraph 78 of the *Critique of Judgment).* Goethe is convinced that man, in his world of ideas, experiences directly how the creative being of nature does things. "When we, in fact, lift ourselves in the moral sphere into a higher region through belief in God, virtue, and immortality and mean to draw near to the primal being, so *likewise, in the intellectual realm, it could very well be the case that we would make ourselves worthy, through beholding an ever-creating nature, of participating spiritually in its productions.* "Man's knowledge is for Goethe a real living into nature's creating and working. It is given to his knowledge "to investigate, to experience *how nature lives in creating."*

It conflicts with the spirit of the Goethean world view to speak of beings that lie outside the world of experience and outside the ideas accessible to the human spirit and that nevertheless are supposed to contain the foundations of this world. All metaphysics are rejected by this world view. There are no questions of knowledge which, rightly posed, cannot also be answered. If science at any given time can make nothing of a certain area of phenomena, then the reason for this does not lie with the nature of the human spirit but rather with the incidental fact that experience of this region is not yet complete at this time. Hypotheses cannot be set up about things that lie outside the region of possible experience but only about things that can sometime enter this region. A hypothesis can always state only that it is likely that within a given region of phenomena one will have this or that experience. In this way of thinking one cannot speak at all about things and processes which do not lie within man's sensible or spiritual view. The assumption of a "thing-in-itself," which causes perceptions in man but which itself can never be perceived, is an inadmissible hypothesis. "Hypotheses are scaffolding that one erects before the building and that one removes when the building is finished; they are indispensable to the workman; only he must not consider the scaffolding to be the building." When confronted by a region of phenomena, for which all perceptions are present and which has been permeated with ideas, the human spirit declares itself satisfied. It feels that within the spirit a living harmony of idea and perception is playing itself out.

The satisfying basic mood that Goethe's world view has for him is similar to that which one can observe with the mystics. Mysticism sets out to find, within the human soul, the primal ground of things, the divinity. The mystic, just like Goethe, is convinced that the being of the world becomes manifest to him in inner experiences. Only, many a mystic does not regard immersion in the world of ideas to be the inner experience that matters the most to him. Many a one-sided mystic has approximately the same view as Kant about the clear ideas of reason. For him they stand outside the creative wholeness of nature and belong only to the human intellect. A mystic of this sort seeks, therefore, by developing unusual states, for example, through ecstasy, to attain the highest knowledge, a vision of a higher kind. He deadens in himself sense observation and the thinking based on reason and seeks to intensify his life of feeling. Then he believes he has a direct feeling of spirituality working in him, as divinity, in fact. He believes that in the moments when he succeeds in this God is living in him. The Goethean world view also arouses a similar feeling in the person who adheres to it. But the Goethean world view does not draw its knowledge from experiences that occur after observation and thinking have been deadened but rather draws them precisely from these two activities. It does not flee to abnormal states of human spiritual life but rather is of the view that the spirit's usual, naive ways of going about things are capable of such perfecting, that man can experience within himself nature's creating. "There are, after all, in the long run, I think, only the practical and self-rectifying operations of man's ordinary intellect that dares to exercise itself in a higher sphere." Many a mystic immerses himself in a world of unclear sensations and feelings; Goethe immerses himself in the clear world of ideas. The one-sided mystics disdain the clarity of ideas. They regard this clarity as superficial. They have no inkling of what those persons sense who have the gift of immersing themselves in the living world of ideas. Such a mystic is chilled when he surrenders himself to the world of ideas. He seeks a world content that radiates warmth. But the content that he finds does not explain the world. It consists only of subjective excitements, in confused mental pictures. Whoever speaks of the coldness of the world of ideas can only *think* ideas, not *experience* them. Whoever lives the true life in the world of ideas, feels in himself the being of the world working in a warmth that cannot be compared to anything else. He feels the fire of the world mystery flame up in him. This is how Goethe felt as there opened up for him in Italy the view of nature at work. Then he knew how that longing is to be stilled which in Frankfurt he has his Faust express with the words:

> Where shall I, endless nature, seize on thee?
> Thy breasts are—where? Ye, of all life the spring,
> To whom both Earth and Heaven cling,
> Toward which the withering breast doth strain.
>
> (Priest's translation)

The Metamorphosis of World Phenomena

Goethe's world view attained its highest level of maturity when there arose for him the view of the two great driving wheels of nature: the significance of the concepts of *polarity* and of *enhancement (Steigerung)*. (See the essay, "Commentary to the Essay *Nature.*") Polarity is characteristic of the phenomena of nature insofar as we think of them as material. It consists of the fact that everything material manifests itself in two opposite states, as the magnet does in a north and a south pole. These states of matter either lie open to view or they slumber in what is material and are able to be wakened by suitable means within it. Enhancement belongs to the phenomena insofar as we think them to be spiritual. It can be observed in processes of nature that fall under the idea of development. At the various levels of development these processes show more or less distinctly in their outer manifestation the idea that underlies them. In the fruit, the idea of the plant, the law of vegetation, is only indistinctly manifest. The idea that the spirit recognizes and the perception are not similar to one another. "In the blossoms the law of vegetation comes into its highest manifestation, and the rose would again be but the pinnacle of the manifestation." What Goethe calls enhancement consists of the bringing forth of the spiritual out of the material by creative nature. That nature is engaged "in an ever-striving ascent" means that it seeks to create forms which, in ascending order, increasingly represent the ideas of things even in outer manifestation. Goethe is of the view that "nature has no secret that it does not somewhere *place naked before the eyes*" of the attentive observer." Nature can bring forth phenomena from which there can be read directly the ideas applicable to a large area of related processes. It is those phenomena in which enhancement has reached its goal, in which the idea becomes immediate truth. The creative spirit of nature comes to the surface of things here; that which, in coarsely material phenomena, can only be grasped by thinking, that which can only be seen with spiritual eyes, becomes, in enhanced phenomena, visible to the physical eye. Everything sense-perceptible is here also spiritual, and everything spiritual is sense-perceptible. Goethe thinks of the whole of nature as permeated by spirit. Its forms are different through the fact that the spirit in them becomes also more or less outwardly visible. Goethe knows no dead, spiritless matter. Those things appear to be so in which the spirit of nature gives an outer form that is not similar to its ideal being. Because *one* spirit works both in nature and in man's inner life, man can lift himself to participation in the productions of nature. "... from the tile that falls from the roof, to the radiant lightning of the spirit that arises in you and that you communicate," everything in the universe is for Goethe an effect, a manifestation of *one* creative spirit. "All the workings we take note of in experience, no matter what their nature, are interconnected in the most consistent way, pass over into one another; they undulate from the first ones to the last." "A tile works loose from the roof: we ordinarily say this happens *by chance;* the tile, after all, certainly strikes the shoulders of a passerby *mechanically;* only, not altogether mechanically: it follows the laws of gravity and thus works *physically*. Ruptured bodily organs cease functioning; at that moment the fluids work *chemically,* the qualities of the elements emerge. But, the interrupted *organic* life reasserts itself just as quickly and seeks to re-establish itself; meanwhile the human entity is more or less unconscious and *psychically* disorganized. The person, regaining consciousness, feels himself *ethically* wounded to the depths; he laments his interrupted activity, no matter of what kind it might be, for no one wants to endure this patiently. *Religiously,* on the other hand, he can easily attribute this case to a higher destiny and regard it as saving him from far greater harm, as leading him to a higher good. This suffices for the sufferer; but the convalescent rises to his feet *highly gifted,* trusts God and himself and feels himself saved, really takes up also what happens by chance, turns it to his advantage, in order to begin an eternally fresh life's cycle." All things working in the world appear to Goethe as modifications of the spirit, and a person who immerses himself in them and observes them, from the level of chance happenings up to that of genius, lives through the metamorphosis of the spirit, from the form in which this spirit presents itself in an outer manifestation not resembling itself, up to the form in which the spirit appears in its own most archetypal form. In the sense of the Goethean world view all creative forces work in a unified way. They are a totality manifesting in successive levels of related manifoldnesses. But Goethe was never inclined to picture the unity of the world to himself as *uniform*. Adherents of the idea of unity often fall into the mistake of extending what can be observed in *one* region of phenomena out over all of nature. The mechanistic world view, for example, is in this situation. It has a particularly good eye and understanding for what can be explained mechanically. Therefore only the mechanical seems to it to be in accordance with nature. It seeks to trace even the phenomena of organic nature back to a mechanical lawfulness. A living thing is for it only a complicated form of the working together of mechanical processes. Goethe found such a world view expressed in a particularly repellent form in Holbach's *Systeme de la Nature,* which came into his hands in Strassburg. One matter supposedly exists from all eternity and has moved for all eternity, and now, with this motion, supposedly brings forth right and left and on all sides, without more ado, the infinite phenomena of existence. "We would indeed have been satisfied with this, if the author had really built up the world before our eyes out of his moving matter. But he might know as little about nature as we do, for as soon as he has staked up a few general concepts, he leaves nature at once, in order to transform what appears as something higher than nature or as a higher nature in nature, into a nature that is material, heavy, moving, to be sure, but still without direction or shape, and he believes that he has gained a great deal by this" *(Poetry and Truth,* second book). Goethe would have expressed himself in a similar way if he could have heard Du Bois-Reymond's statement *(Limits to Knowing Nature,* page 13): "Knowledge of nature ... is a tracing of the changes in the corporeal world back to the movements of atoms that are caused by their central forces, independent of time, or it is a dissolving of all the processes of nature into the *mechanics of the atom."* Goethe thought the different kinds of nature workings to be related to each other and as passing over into one another; but he never wanted to trace them back to one single kind. He was not striving for one abstract principle to which all the phenomena of nature should be traced, but rather he strove for observation of the characteristic way in which creative nature manifested its general lawfulness in particular forms within every single one of its realms. He did not want to force *one* thought form upon the whole of nature's phenomena, but rather, by living into the different thought forms, he wanted to keep his spirit as lively and pliable as nature itself is. When the feeling of the great unity of all nature's working was powerful in him, then he was a pantheist. "I for myself, with all the manifold tendencies of my nature, cannot get enough from one way of thinking; as poet and artist I am a polytheist, as natural scientist a pantheist, and am one just as positively as the other. If I need a God for my personality as a moral person, that is also already provided for" (to Jacobi, January 6, 1813). As artist, Goethe turned to those phenomena of nature in which the idea is present to direct perception. The single thing appeared here directly as divine; the world as a multiplicity of divine individualities. As natural scientist Goethe had to follow the forces of nature also into phenomena whose idea does not become visible in its individual existence. As poet he could be at peace with himself about the multiplicity of the divine; as natural scientist he had to seek the ideas of nature, which worked in a unified way. "The law, that comes into manifestation in the greatest freedom, in accordance with its most archetypal conditions, brings forth what is objectively beautiful, which, to be sure, must find worthy subjects by whom it can be grasped." This objectively beautiful within the individual creature is what Goethe as artist wants to behold; but as natural scientist he wants "to know the laws according to which universal nature wants to act." Polytheism is the way of thinking that sees and reveres something spiritual in the single thing; pantheism is the other way, which grasps the spirit of the whole. Both ways of thinking can exist side by side; the one or the other comes into play according to whether one's gaze is directed upon nature's wholeness, which is life and sequence out of a center, or upon those individuals in which nature unites in *one* form what it as a rule spreads out over a whole realm. Such forms arise when, for example, the creative forces of nature, after "thousandfold plants," make yet one more, in which "all the others are contained," or "after thousandfold animals make one being which contains them all: *man.*"

Goethe once made the remark: "Whoever has learned to understand them (my writings) and my nature in general will have to admit after all that he has won a certain inner freedom" (Conversations with Chancellor F. von Mueller, January 5, 1831). With this he was pointing to the working power that comes into play in all human striving to know. As long as man stops short at perceiving the antitheses around him and at regarding their laws as principles implanted in them by which they are governed, he has the feeling that they confront him as unknown powers, which work upon him and impose upon him the thoughts of their laws. He feels himself to be unfree with respect to the things; he experiences the lawfulness of nature as rigid necessity into which he must fit himself. Only when man becomes aware that the forces of nature are nothing other than forms of the same spirit that also works in himself does the insight arise in him that he does partake of freedom. The lawfulness of nature is experienced as compelling only as long as one regards it as an alien power. Living into its being, one experiences it as a power that one also exercises in one's own inner life; one experiences oneself as a productive element; working along with the becoming and being of things. One is on intimate terms with any power that has to do with becoming. One has taken up into one's own doing what one otherwise experiences only as outer incentive. This is the process of liberation that is effected by the act of knowledge, in the sense of the Goethean world view. Goethe clearly perceived the ideas of nature's working as he encountered them in Italian works or art. He had a clear experience also of the liberating effect that the possession of these ideas has upon man. A result of this experience is his description of that kind of knowledge that he characterizes as that of *encompassing* individuals. "The encompassing ones, whom one in a prouder sense could call the creative ones, conduct themselves productively in the highest sense; insofar, namely, as they take their start from ideas, they express already the unity of the whole, *and afterward it is in a certain way up to nature to fit in with this idea."* But Goethe never got to the point of having a direct view of the act of liberation itself. Only that person can have this view who in his knowing is attentive to himself. Goethe, to be sure, practiced the highest kind of knowledge; but he did not observe this kind of knowledge in himself. He admits to himself, after all:

"How did you get so very far?
They say you have done it all wonderfully well!"
My child! In this I have been smart;
I have never thought about thinking at all.

But just as the creative nature forces, "after thousandfold plants," make yet one more in which "all the others are contained," so do they also, after thousandfold ideas, bring forth yet one more in which the whole world of ideas is contained. And man grasps this idea when, to his perception of the other things and processes he adds that of thinking as well. Just because Goethe's thinking was continuously filled with the objects of perception, because his thinking was a perceiving, his perceiving a thinking, he could not come to the point of making thinking itself into an object of thinking. One attains the idea of freedom, however, only by looking at thinking. Goethe did not make the distinction between thinking about thinking and *looking at thinking*. Otherwise he would have attained the insight that one, precisely in the sense of *his* world view, could very well reject thinking about thinking, but that one could nevertheless come to *a beholding of* the thought world. Man is uninvolved in the coming about of everything else he sees. The ideas of what he sees arise in him. But these ideas would not be there if there were not present in him the productive power to bring them to manifestation. Even though ideas are the content of what *works* within the things, they come into manifest existence through human activity. Man can therefore know the intrinsic nature of the world of ideas only if he looks at his activity. With everything else he sees he penetrates only into the idea at work in it; the thing, in which the idea works, remains as perception outside of his spirit. When he looks at the idea, what is working and what is brought forth are both entirely contained within his inner life. He has the entire process totally present in his inner life. What he sees no longer appears as brought forth by the idea; for what he sees is itself now idea. To see something bringing forth itself is, however, to see freedom. In observing his thinking man sees into world happening. Here he does not have to search for an idea of this happening, because this happening is the idea itself. What one otherwise experiences as the unity of what is looked at and the ideas is here the experiencing of the spirituality of the world of ideas become visible. The person who beholds this self-sustaining activity feels freedom. Goethe in fact *experienced* this feeling, but did not express it in its highest form. In his looking at nature he *exercised* a free activity, but this activity never became an object of perception for him. He never saw behind the scenes of human knowing and therefore never took up into his consciousness the idea of world happening in its most archetypal form, in its highest metamorphosis. As soon as a person attains a view of this metamorphosis, he then conducts himself with sureness in the realm of things. In the center of his personality he has won the true starting point for all consideration of the world. He will no longer search for unknown foundations, for the causes lying outside him, of things; he knows that the highest experience of which he is capable consists of self-contemplation of his own being. Whoever is completely permeated with the feelings that this experience calls forth will gain the truest relationships to things. A person for whom this is not the case will seek the highest form of existence elsewhere, and, since he cannot find it within experience, will suppose it to be in an unknown region of reality. Uncertainty will enter into his considerations of things; in answering the questions that nature poses him, he will continually call upon something he cannot investigate. Because, through his life in the world of ideas, Goethe had *a feeling* of the firm center within his personality, he succeeded, within certain limits, in arriving at sure concepts in his contemplation of nature. But because he lacked a direct view of his innermost experiences, he groped about uncertainly outside these limits. For this reason he says that man is not born "to solve the problems of the world but in fact to seek where the problem begins, and then to keep oneself within the limits of what is understandable." He says, "Kant has unquestionably been of most use in his drawing of the limits to which the human spirit is capable of penetrating, and through the fact that he let unsolvable problems lie." If a view of man's highest experience had given him certainty in his contemplation of things, then he would have been able to do more along his path than "through regulated experience, to attain a kind of qualified trustworthiness." Instead of proceeding straight ahead through his experiences in the consciousness that the true has significance only insofar as it is demanded by human nature, he still arrives at the conviction that a *"higher influence* helps those who are steadfast, active, understanding, disciplined and disciplining, humane, devout" and that "the moral world order" manifests itself most beautifully where it "comes indirectly to the aid of the good person, of the courageously suffering person."

*

Because Goethe did not know the innermost human experience, it was not possible for him to attain the ultimate thoughts about the moral world order that necessarily belong to his view of nature. The ideas of the things are the content of what works and creates within the things. Man experiences moral ideas directly in the form of ideas. Whoever is able to experience how, in his beholding of the world of ideas, the ideal element itself becomes content, fills itself with itself, is also in a position to experience the production of the moral within human nature. Whoever knows the ideas of nature only in their relation to the world we behold will also want to relate moral concepts to something external to them. He will seek for these concepts a reality similar to that which is present for concepts won from experience. But whoever is able to view ideas in their most essential being will become aware, with moral ideas, that nothing external corresponds to them, that they are directly produced as ideas in spiritual experience. It is clear to him that neither a divine will, working only outwardly, nor a moral world order of a like sort are at work to produce these ideas. For there is in them nothing to be seen of any relation to such powers. Everything they express is also contained within their spiritually experienced pure idea-form. Only through their own content do they work upon man as moral powers. No categorical imperative stands behind them with a whip forcing man to follow them. Man feels that *he* has brought them forth and loves them the way one loves one's child. Love is the motive of his action. The spiritual pleasure in one's own creation is the source of the moral.

There are people who are unable to produce any moral ideas. They take up into themselves the moral ideas of other people through tradition, and if they have no ability to behold ideas as such, they do not recognize the origin, experienceable in the spirit, of the moral. They seek it in a supra-human will outside themselves. Or they believe that there exists, outside the spirit world which man experiences, an objective moral world order from which the moral ideas stem. The speech organ of that world order is often sought in the conscience of man. As with certain things in the rest of his world view, Goethe is also uncertain in his thoughts about the origin of the moral. Here also his feeling for what is in accord with ideas brings forth statements that are in accord with the demands of his nature. "Duty: where one loves what one commands oneself to do." Only a person who sees the foundations of the moral purely in the content of moral ideas should say: "Lessing, who resentfully felt many a limitation, has one of his characters say, 'No one has to have to.' A witty jovial man said, 'Whoever wants to has to.' A third, admittedly a cultivated person, added, 'Whoever has insight, also wants to.' And in this way it was believed that the whole circle of knowing, wanting, and having to had been closed. But in the average case, man's *knowledge,* no matter what kind it is, determines what he does or doesn't do; for this reason there is also nothing worse than to see ignorance in action." The following statement shows that in Goethe a feeling for the true nature of the moral held sway, but did not rise into clear view: "In order to perfect itself the will must, in its moral life, give itself over to conscience which does not err . . . Conscience needs no *ancestor;* with conscience everything is given; it has to do only with one's own inner world." To state that conscience needs no ancestor can only mean that man does not originally find within himself any moral content; he gives this content to himself. Other statements stand in contrast to these, setting the origin of the moral into a region ouside man: "Man, no matter how much the earth attracts him with its thousand upon thousand manifestations, nevertheless lifts up his gaze longingly toward heaven ... because he feels deeply and clearly within himself that he is a citizen of that spiritual realm which we are not able to deny nor give up our belief." "We leave to God, as the *all-determining* and all-liberating Being, what is totally insoluble."

*

Goethe lacks the organ for the contemplation of man's innermost nature, for self-perception. "I hereby confess that from the beginning the great and significant sounding task, *know thou thyself,* has always seemed suspect to me, as a ruse of secretly united priests who wanted to confuse man with unattainable demands and to seduce him away from activity in the outer world into an inner false contemplation. Man knows himself only insofar as he knows the world that he becomes aware of only within himself and himself only within it. Every new object that we really look at opens up a new organ within us." Exactly the reverse of this is true: man knows the world only insofar as he knows himself. For in his inner life there reveals itself in its most archetypal form what is present to view in outer things only in reflection, in example, symbol. What man otherwise can only speak of as something unfathomable, undiscoverable, divine, comes into view in its true form in self-perception. Because in self-perception he sees what is ideal in its direct form, he gains the strength and ability to seek out and recognize this ideal element also in all outer phenomena, in the whole of nature. Someone who has experienced the moment of self-perception no longer thinks in terms of seeking some "hidden" God behind phenomena: he grasps the divine in its different metamorphoses in nature. Goethe remarked, with respect to

Schelling: "I would see him more often if I did not still hope for poetic moments; philosophy destroys poetry for me, and does so for the good reason that it drives me to the object because I can never remain purely speculative but must seek right away a perception for every principle and therefore flee right away out into nature." He was in fact not able to find the highest perception, the perception of the world of ideas itself. This perception cannot destroy poetry, for it only frees one's spirit from all supposition that there might be an unknown, unfathomable something in nature. But for this reason it makes him capable of giving himself over entirely, without preconceptions, to things; for it gives him the conviction that everything can be drawn from nature that the spirit can ever want from it.

But this highest perception liberates man's spirit also from all one-sided feeling of dependency. He feels himself, through having this view, to be sovereign in the realm of the moral world order. He knows that the driving power that brings forth everything works in his inner life as within his own will, and that the highest decisions about morality lie within himself. For these highest decisions flow out of the world of moral ideas, in whose production the soul of man is present. Even though a person may feel himself restricted in part, may also be dependent upon a thousand things, on the whole he sets himself his moral goal and his moral direction. What is at work in all other things comes to manifestation in the human being as idea; what is at work in him is the idea that he himself brings forth. In every single human individuality a process occurs that plays itself out in the whole of nature: the creation of something actual out of the idea. And the human being himself is the creator. For upon the foundation of his personality there lives the idea that gives a content to itself. Going beyond Goethe one must broaden his principle that nature is "great enough in the wealth of its creation to make, after thousandfold plants, *one* in which all the others are contained, and to make, after thousandfold animals, *one* being that contains them all: man. "Nature is so great in its creation that it repeats in every human individual the process by which it brings forth freely out of the idea all creatures, repeats it through the fact that moral actions spring from the ideal foundation of the personality. Whatever a person also feels to be an objective reason for his action is only a transcribing and at the same time a mistaking of his own being. The human being realizes himself in his moral actions. Max Stirner has expressed this knowledge in lapidary words in his book, *The Single Individual and What Is His Own.* "It lies in my power to be my own person, and this is so when I know myself as a *single individual.* Within the *single individual* even someone who is his own person returns to the creative nothingness out of which he is born. Every higher being over me, be it God or man, weakens the feeling of my singleness and pales only before the sun of this consciousness. If I base my affairs upon myself, the single individual, then they rest upon their own transitory mortal creator, who devours himself, and I can say that I have based my affairs upon nothing." But at the same time one can tell this Stirnerian spirit what Faust told Mephistopheles: "In your nothingness I hope to find my all," for there dwells in my inner life in an individual form the working power by which nature creates the universe. As long as a person has not beheld this working power within himself, he will appear with respect to it the way Faust did with respect to the earth spirit. This working power will always call out to him the words, "You resemble the spirit that you can grasp, not me!" Only the beholding of one's deepest inner life conjures up this spirit, who says of itself:

> In the tides of life, in action's storm,
> Up and down I wave,
> To and fro weave free,
> Birth and the grave,
> An infinite sea,
> A varied weaving,

A radiant living,
Thus at Time's humming loom it's my hand that prepares
The robe ever-living the Deity wears.

                                      (Priest's translation)

    I have tried to present in my *Philosophy of Spiritual Activity* how knowledge of the fact that man in his doing is based upon himself comes from the most inward experience, from the beholding of his own being. In 1844 Stirner defended the view that man, if he truly understands himself, can see only in himself the basis for his activity. With Stirner, however, this knowledge does not arise from a beholding of his innermost experience but rather from the *feeling* of freedom and independence from all world powers that require coercion. Stirner stops short at *demanding* freedom; he is led in this area to put the bluntest possible emphasis upon the human nature that is based upon itself. I am trying to describe the life in freedom on a broader basis, by showing what man sees when he looks into the foundation of his soul. Goethe did not go as far as to behold freedom, because he had an antipathy for self-knowledge. If that had not been the case, then knowledge of man as a free personality founded upon himself would have had to be the peak of his world view. The germ of this knowledge is to be found everywhere in his works; it is at the same time the germ of his view of nature. In his actual nature studies Goethe never speaks of unexplorable foundations, of hidden driving powers of phenomena. He contents himself with observing the phenomena in their sequence and of explaining them with the help of those elements which, during observation, reveal themselves to the senses and to the spirit. In this vein he writes to Jacobi on May 5, 1786 that he has the courage "to devote his whole life to the contemplation of the things that he can hope to reach" and of whose being "he can hope to form an adequate idea," without bothering himself in the least about how far he will get and about what is cut out for him. A person who believes he can draw near to the divine in the individual objects of nature no longer needs to form a particular mental picture for himself of a God that exists outside of and beside the things. It is only when Goethe leaves the realm of nature that his feeling for the being of things no longer holds up. Then his lack of human self-knowledge leads him to make assertions that are reconcilable neither with his inborn way of thinking nor with the direction of his nature studies. Someone who is inclined to cite these assertions might assume that Goethe believed in an anthropomorphic God and in the individual continuation of that life-form of the soul which is bound up with the conditions of the physical bodily organization. Such a belief stands in contradiction to Goethe's nature studies. They could never have taken the direction they did if in them Goethe had allowed himself to be determined by this belief. It lies totally in the spirit of his nature studies to think the being of the human soul such that, after laying aside the body, it lives in a supersensible form of existence. This form of existence requires that the soul, because of different life requirements, also take on a different kind of consciousness from the one it has through the physical body. In this way the Goethean teaching of metamorphosis leads also to the view of metamorphoses of soul life. But this Goethean idea of immortality can be regarded correctly only if one knows that Goethe had not been able to be led by his world view to an unmetamorphosed continuation of that spiritual life that is determined by the physical body. Because Goethe, in the sense indicated here, did not attempt to view his life of thought, he was also not moved in his further life's course to develop particularly this idea of immortality that would be the continuation of his thoughts on metamorphosis. *This* idea, however, would in truth be what would follow from his world view with respect to this region of knowledge. Whatever expression he gave to a personal feeling about the view of life of this or that contemporary, or out of any other motivation, without his thinking thereby of the connection to the world view won through his nature studies, may not be brought forward as characteristic of Goethe's idea of immortality.

For the evaluation of a Goethean statement within the total picture of his world view there also comes into consideration the fact that his mood of soul in his different stages of life gives particular nuances to such statements. He was fully conscious of these changes in the form of expression of his ideas. When Foerster expressed the view that the solution to the Faust problem is to be found in the words, "A good man is in his dim impulse well aware of his right path," Goethe responded, "That would be rationalism. Faust ends up as an old man, and in old age we become mystics." And in his prose aphorisms we read, "A certain philosophy answers to each age of man. The child appears as realist; for he finds himself as convinced of the existence of pears and apples as of his own. The youth, assailed by inner passions, must take notice of himself, feel his way forward; he is transformed into an idealist. On the other hand the grown man has every reason to become a skeptic; he does well to doubt whether the means he has chosen for his purpose are indeed the right ones. Before acting and in acting he has every reason to keep his intellect mobile, so that afterward he does not have to feel badly about a wrong choice. The old man, however, will always adhere to mysticism; he sees that so much seems to depend upon chance; what is unreasonable succeeds; what is reasonable goes amiss; fortune and misfortune turn unexpectedly into the same thing; it is so, it was so, and old age attains peace in what is, what was, and will be."

I am focusing in this book upon the world view of Goethe out of which his insights into the life of nature have grown and which was the driving force in him from his discovery of the intermaxillary bone in man up to the completion of his studies on color. And I believe I have shown that *this* world view corresponds more perfectly to the total personality of Goethe than does any compilation of statements in which one would have to take into account how such thoughts are colored by the mood of his youthful period or by that of his old age. I believe that Goethe in his studies of nature, although not guided by a clear self-knowledge in accord with ideas, was guided by a right feeling and did observe *a free* way of working that flowed from a true relationship between human nature and the outer world. Goethe is himself clear about the fact that there is something incomplete about his way of thinking: "I was aware of having great and noble purposes *but could never understand the determining factors under which I worked;* I was well aware of what I lacked, and likewise of what I had too much of; therefore I did not cease to develop myself, outwardly and from within. And still it was as before. I pursued every purpose with earnestness, force, and faithfulness; in doing so I often succeeded in completely overcoming stubborn conditions but also often foundered because I could not learn to give in and to go around. And so my life went by this way, in doing and enjoying, in suffering and resisting, in the love, contentment, hatred, and disapproval of others. Find yourself mirrored here whoever's destiny was the same."

II

Goethe's Views on the Nature and Development of Living Beings

Metamorphosis

Goethe's relationship to the natural sciences cannot be understood if one confines oneself merely to the single discoveries he made. I consider the words that Goethe addressed to Knebel on August 18, 1787 from Italy to be the guiding point of view in looking at this relationship: "To judge by the plants and fish I have seen in Naples and Sicily, I would, if I were ten years younger, *be tempted to make a trip to India, not in order to discover something new but rather in order to contemplate in my own way what has already been discovered.*" What seems most significant to me is the way in which Goethe drew together the phenomena of nature known to him into a view of nature that accorded with his way of thinking. If all the single discoveries he succeeded in making had already been made before him, and if he had given us nothing more than his *view of nature,* this would not lessen the significance of his nature studies in the slightest. I agree with Du Bois-Reymond that "even without Goethe, science would be just as far along as it is," that the steps he took would sooner or later have been taken by others *(Goethe and More Goethe).* Only I cannot extend these words, as Du Bois-Reymond does, to include the whole of Goethe's natural scientific work. I limit them to the single discoveries he made in the course of it. All of these discoveries would probably have been made by now even if Goethe had never concerned himself with botany, anatomy, etc. His view of nature, however, is an outgrowth of his personality; no one else could have come to it. Goethe's individual discoveries also did not interest him. During his studies they forced themselves upon him of their own accord, because certain views held sway in his time about facts relating to these discoveries, which were incompatible with his way of looking at things. If he had been able with what natural science provided him to build up his view, then he would never have occupied himself with study of the details. He had to go into the particulars because what was told him about the particulars by natural scientists did not meet his requirements. And only by chance, as it were, did the individual discoveries result from these studies of the details. He was not primarily concerned with the question as to whether man, like the other animals, has an intermaxillary bone in the upper jaw. He wanted to discover the ground-plan by which nature forms the sequence of animals and, at the highest level of this succession, forms man. He wanted to find the common archetype that underlies all species of animals and that finally, in its highest perfection, also underlies the human species. The natural scientists said to him that there is a difference between the structure of an animal's body and that of man. The animals have an intermediary bone in the upper jaw, and man does not have it. But his view was that man's physical structure could differ from that of the animal only in its degree of perfection but not in particulars. For, if the latter were the case, then a common archetype could not underlie both the animal and the human organization. Goethe could do nothing with this assertion of the natural scientists. Therefore he looked for the intermediary bone in man and found it. Something similar can be observed in all his individual discoveries. They are never for him a purpose in themselves. They must be made in order to show that his picture of the phenomena of nature is valid.

In the area of organic natural phenomena the significant thing about Goethe's view is the mental picture he developed of the *nature of life*. The main thing is not his emphasis upon the fact that leaf, calyx, corolla, etc., are organs of the plant that are identical to each other and that develop from a common basic structure; the main thing is what mental picture Goethe had of the whole of plant nature as something living and how he thought of the particulars as coming forth out of this whole. His idea of the *nature of the organism* has to be called his most original and central discovery in the area of biology. Goethe's basic conviction was that something can be seen in the plant and in the animal that is not accessible to mere sense observation. What the bodily eye can observe about the organism seems to Goethe to be only the result of the living whole of developmental laws working through one another and accessible to the *spiritual eye* alone. What he saw about the plant and the animal with his spiritual eye is what he described. Only someone who is as capable of seeing as he was can think through his idea of the nature of the organism. Whoever stops short at what the senses and experiments provide cannot understand Goethe. When we read his two poems, the *Metamorphosis of the Plants* and the *Metamorphosis of the Animals,* it seems at first as though his words only lead us from one part of the organism to another, as though things of a merely external, factual nature are meant to be connected. But if we permeate ourselves with what hovered before Goethe as idea of the living being, we then feel ourselves carried into the sphere of the living organic, and the mental pictures of the individual organs grow out of one central mental picture.

*

As Goethe began to think independently about the phenomena of nature, the *concept of life* occupied his attention above all else. In a letter of July 14, 1770 from his Strassburg period, he writes about a butterfly: "The poor creature trembles in the net, rubs off its most beautiful colors; and even if one captures it unharmed, it lies there finally stiff and lifeless; the corpse is not the whole creature; something else belongs to it, a main part still, and in this case as in every other a most major main part: *its life."* The fact that an organism cannot be regarded as a dead product of nature, that there is still more in it than the forces that also live in inorganic nature, was clear to Goethe from the beginning. Du Bois-Reymond is undoubtedly right when he states that "the constructing of a purely mechanical world, of which science consists today, would not have been less hated by the poet prince of Weimar than the 'systeme de la nature' once was by Friederike's friend"; and he is no less right with his other statement that *"Goethe would have turned away shuddering from this world construct which, through its spontaneous generation, borders on the Kant-Laplace theory, from the view that man arose out of chaos through the mathematically determined play of atoms from eternity to eternity, from the ending of the world in freezing cold, from all these pictures that our generation looks so unfeelingly in the face, just as it has grown used to the horrors of railroad travel" (Goethe and More Goethe)*. For sure, he would have turned away shuddering, because he sought, and also found, a higher concept of the living than that of a complicated mathematically determined mechanism. Only someone who is incapable of grasping a higher concept such as this and who identifies the living with the mechanical because he is able to see in the organism only the mechanical, only he will warm to the mechanical construct of the world and its play of atoms and will look unfeelingly upon the pictures that Du Bois-Reymond conjures up. But someone who can take up into himself the concept of the organic in Goethe's sense will quarrel just as little about its validity as he will about the existence of the mechanical. One does not quarrel, after all, with the color-blind about the world of colors. All views which picture as mechanical what is organic fall under the judgment which Goethe has Mephistopheles make:

> Who'll know aught living and describe it well,
> Seeks first the spirit to expel.
> He then has the component parts in hand
> But lacks, alas! the spirit's band.
>   (Priest's translation)

*

Goethe found it possible to occupy himself more intimately with the life of the plants when Duke Karl August presented him with a garden on April 21, 1776. Goethe was also stimulated by his walks in the Thueringen forest, on which he could observe how the life of the lower organisms manifested itself. The mosses and lichens drew his attention. On October 31 he asked Frau von Stein for mosses of all kinds, damp and with roots where possible, so that he could use them to observe their propagation. It is important to keep in mind the fact that Goethe, at the beginning of his botanical studies, occupied himself with the lower plant forms. For later, in conceiving his idea of the archetypal plant, he only took into account the higher plants. His doing so cannot therefore be due to the fact that the realm of the lower plants was unfamiliar to him, but rather was due to the fact that he believed the secrets of the plant's nature to be more distinct and pronounced in the higher plants. He wanted to seek out the idea of nature where it revealed itself most clearly and then to descend from the perfect to the imperfect, in order to understand the latter by the former. He did not want to explain what is complex by what is simple, but rather he wanted, with *one* look, to have an overview of what is complex as a working whole, and then explain what is simple and imperfect as a one-sided development out of what is complex and perfect. If nature is able, after innumerable plant forms, to make yet one more that contains them all, then also, as the spirit beholds this perfect form, the secret of plant development must be revealed to it in direct beholding, and it will then be able easily to apply what it has observed about what is perfect to what is imperfect. The natural scientists do it the other way around; they consider what is perfect to be only the mechanical sum total of simple processes. They start with what is simple and derive what is perfect from it.

As Goethe looked around for a scientific guide for his botanical studies, he could find none except Linnaeus. We first hear about his study of Linnaeus in his letters to Frau von Stein in the year 1782. The interest he took in Linnaeus' books shows how serious Goethe was about his natural scientific strivings. He admits that, aside from Shakespeare and Spinoza, Linnaeus had the greatest effect upon him. But how little Linnaeus was able to satisfy him. Goethe wanted to observe the different plant forms in order to recognize the common element living in them. He wanted to know what made all these forms into plants. And Linnaeus had been content to place the manifold plant forms next to one another in a particular order and to describe them. Here in an individual case Goethe's naive, unprejudiced observation of nature ran up against science's way of thinking that was influenced by a one-sidedly understood Platonism. This way of thinking sees in the individual forms realizations of the archetypal Platonic ideas or thoughts of the creation, existing alongside one another. Goethe sees in each individual form only one particular development out of one ideal archetypal being which lives in all forms. The first way of thinking wants to distinguish as exactly as possible the individual forms in order to recognize the manifold nature of idea-forms or of the plan of creation; Goethe wants to explain the manifold nature of the particulars out of their original unity. The fact that very much exists in manifold forms is immediately clear to the first way of thinking, because to it the ideal archetypes are already what is manifold. For Goethe this is not clear, since the many belong together, in his view, only if a *oneness* reveals itself in them. Goethe says, therefore, that what Linnaeus "sought forcibly to keep apart had to strive for unity, in accordance with the innermost need of my being." Linnaeus simply accepts the existing forms without asking how they have come into being out of a basic form: "We can count as many species as there have been different forms created in principle": this is his basic tenet. Goethe seeks what is working in the plant realm and creating the individual plants by bringing forth specific forms out of the basic form.

Goethe found in Rousseau a more naive relationship to the plant world than in Linnaeus. On June 16, 1782 he wrote to Karl August: "Among Rousseau's works there are some most delightful letters about botany, in which he presents this science to a lady in a most comprehensible and elegant way. It is a real model of how one should teach, and it supplements *Emil.* I use it therefore as an excuse to recommend anew the beautiful realm of the flowers to my beautiful lady friends." In his *History of My Botanical Studies* Goethe sets forth what it was that drew him to Rousseau's botanical ideas: "His relationship to plant lovers and connoisseurs, especially to the Duchess of Portland, could have given his sharp eye more breadth of vision, and a spirit like his, which feels itself called upon to proscribe order and lawfulness to the nations had, after all, *to gain an inkling that such a great diversity of forms could not appear within the immeasurable realm of the plants, unless one basic law, no matter how hidden it may also be, brought all these forms back into unity."* Goethe also sought just such a basic law as this which brings the diversity back into the unity from which it originally went forth.

Two books of Baron von Gleichen, called Russwurm, appeared back then on Goethe's spiritual horizon. They both treat the life of the plants in a way that could become fruitful for him: *The Latest News from the Plant Realm* (Nuernberg, 1764) and *Special Microscopic Discoveries about Plants* (Nuernberg, 1777-1781). They concern themselves with the fructification processes of plants. In them pollen, stamens, and pistil are carefully described, and the processes of fructification are presented in well-executed diagrams. Goethe now makes experiments himself in order to observe with his own eyes the results described by von Gleichen-Russwurm. On January 12, 1785 he writes to Jacobi: "A microscope is set up in order, when spring arrives, to reobserve and verify the experiments of von

Gleichen, called Russwurm." At the same time he studies the nature of the seed, as we can tell from a report to Kniebel on April 2, 1785: "I have thought through the substance of the seed as far as my experiences reach." These observations of Goethe's appear in the right light only when one takes into account that already then he did not stop short at them, but rather sought to gain a complete view of the processes of nature for which they were meant to serve as supports and substantiation. On April 8 of the same year he announces to Merck that he had not only observed the facts but had also "combined" these facts "nicely."

*

An essential influence on the development of Goethe's ideas about the organic workings of nature was his participation in Lavater's great work, *Physiognomical Fragments for Furthering Human Knowledge and Human Love,* which appeared in the years 1775-1778. He himself made contributions to this work. In the way he expresses himself in these contributions, his later way of regarding the organic is already prefigured. Lavater stopped short at dealing with the shape of the human organism as an expression of the soul. From the forms of bodies he wanted to read the characters of souls. Goethe began, even back then, to look upon the outer shape for its own sake and to study its own lawfulness and power of development. He occupies himself at the same time with the writings of Aristotle on physiognomy and attempts, on the basis of a study of organic form, to determine the difference between man and animals. He finds this difference in the way the whole human structure brings the head into prominence and in the perfect development of the human brain toward which all the other parts point as though to an organ to which they are attuned. On the other hand, with the animals the head is merely hung upon the spine; the brain and spinal cord have no more scope than is absolutely necessary for carrying out the lower instinctual life and for directing purely physical processes. Goethe sought already back then the difference between man and the animals, not in one or another detail but rather in the different level of perfection that the same basic form attains in the one or other case. There already hovered before him the picture of a prototype that is to be found both in the animals and in man, which is developed in the former in such a way that the whole structure serves animal functions, whereas in the latter the structure provides the basic framework for the development of spirit.

Goethe's special study of anatomy grows out of such considerations. On January 22, 1776 he lets Lavater know that "The duke had six skulls sent to me; have noticed some marvelous things that are at your honor's service, if you have not found them without me." In Goethe's diary we read, under the October 15, 1781 date, that he studied anatomy with old Einsiedel in Jena and in the same year began to have Loder introduce him to this science in a more detailed way. He tells of this in letters to Frau von Stein on October 29, 1781 and to the Duke on November 4. He also has the intention of "explaining the skeleton" to the young people in the Art Academy, and of introducing them to a knowledge of the human body. "I do it," he says, "for my sake and for theirs; the methods I have chosen will make them, over this winter, fully familiar with the basic pillars of the body." One can tell from his diary that he also did give these lectures. Around this time he also had many conversations with Loder about the structure of the human body. And again it is his general view of nature that appears as the driving force and actual goal of these studies. He treats the "bones as a text to which all life and everything human can be appended" (letter to Lavater and Merck, November 14, 1781). Mental pictures about how the organic works, about the connection of human form with animal form, occupy his spirit at that time. The idea that the human structure is only the highest level of the animal one and that man, through this more perfect stage of animal structure, brings forth the moral world out of himself, this is an idea already incorporated into the ode, "The Divine," from the year 1782.

> Noble be man,
> Helpful and good!
> For that *alone*
> Distinguishes him
> From all the beings
> That we know.
>
> By iron laws
> Mighty, eternal,
> Must we all
> Round off our
> Circle of life.

The "eternal iron laws" work in man in exactly the same way as in the rest of the world of organisms; only they attain in him a perfection through which it is possible for him to be "noble, helpful, and good." While in Goethe such ideas as these were taking ever deeper root, Herder was working on his *Ideas on a Philosophy of the History of Mankind.* All the thoughts in this book were talked through by both men. Goethe was satisfied by Herder's conception of nature. It coincided with his own picture. "Herder's book makes it likely that we were first plants and animals ... Goethe is now digging very thoughtfully in these things, and each thing that has once passed through his mind becomes extremely interesting," Frau von Stein writes to Knebel on May 1, 1784. The words that Goethe addresses to Knebel on December 8, 1783 show how very much one is justified in judging from Herder's ideas what Goethe's were: "Herder is writing a philosophy of history, as you can imagine, new from the ground up. We read the first chapters together the day before yesterday;

they are exquisite." Sentences like the following are entirely in the direction of Goethe's thinking. "The human race is the great confluence of lower organic forces." "And so we can assume the fourth principle: *that man is a central creation among the animals, i. e., that he is the form worked through in which the traits of all the species gather around him in their finest essence.*"

To be sure, this picture was irreconcilable with the view of the anatomists of that time that the small bone that animals have in the upper jaw, the intermaxillary bone that holds the upper incisors, was lacking in man. Soemmering, one of the most significant anatomists of his day, wrote to Merck on October 8, 1782: "I wish you had consulted Blumenbach on the subject of the intermaxillary bone which, other things being equal, is the only bone that all animals have, from the ape on, including even the orangutan, but that is *never* found in man; except for this bone there is nothing keeping you from being able to transfer everything man has onto the animals. I enclose therefore the head of a *doe* in order to convince you that this *os intermaxillare*" (as Blumenbach calls it) or *"os incisivum"* (as Camper calls it) is present even in animals that have no incisors in the upper jaw." That was the general opinion of the time. Even the famous Camper, for whom Merck and Goethe had the deepest respect, adhered to this view. The fact that man's intermaxillary bone is ingrown, left and right, to the upper jaw bone without there being visible any clear line there in a normally developed individual led to this view. If the scholars had been right in this view, then it would be impossible to set up a common archetype for the structure of the animal and of the human organism; a boundary between the two forms would have to be assumed. Man would not be created according to the archetype that also underlies the animals. Goethe had to clear away this obstacle to his world view. He succeeded in this in the spring of 1784 in collaboration with Loder. Goethe proceeded in accordance with his general principle, "that nature has no secret that it does not somewhere present openly to the eye of an attentive observer." He found in some abnormally developed skulls that the line between the intermaxillary bone and the upper jaw bone was actually present. On March 27 he joyfully announced his find to Herder and Frau von Stein. To Herder he writes: "It should heartily please you also, *for it is like the keystone to man;* it is not lacking; it is there too! And how! *I thought of it also in connection with your whole picture,* how beautiful it will be there." And when, in November 1784, Goethe sends the treatise he has written about the matter to Kriebel, he indicates the significance for his whole picture of the world that he attaches to the discovery with the words: "I have refrained from showing yet the result, to which Herder already points in his ideas, which is, namely, that one cannot find the difference between man and animal in the details." Goethe could gain confidence in his view of nature only when the erroneous view about this fateful little bone was cleared away. He gradually gained the courage to "extend over all realms of nature, over its entire realm" his ideas about the way nature, playing as it were with *one* main form, brings forth its manifold life. He writes in this vein to Frau von Stein in the year 1786.

*

The book of nature becomes ever more legible to Goethe after he has correctly deciphered this one letter. "My long efforts at spelling have helped me; now suddenly it is working, and my quiet joy is inexpressible," he writes to Frau von Stein on May 15, 1785. He now considers himself already able to write a small botanical treatise for Knebel. The trip to Karlsbad that he undertakes with Knebel in 1785 turns into a journey of formal botanical studies. Upon his return the realms of mushrooms, mosses, lichens, and algae are gone through with reference to Linnaeus. On November 9 he shares with Frau von Stein that "I continue to read Linnaeus; I have to; I have no other book with me. It is the best way to read a book thoroughly, a way I must often practice, especially since I do not easily read a book to the end. This one, however, is not principally made for reading but rather for review, and it serves me now excellently, since I have thought over most of its points myself." During these studies the basic form, from which nature produces all the varied plant shapes, also takes on some outlines in his spirit even though they are not yet clear ones. A letter to Frau von Stein on July 9, 1786 contains the words: "It is a becoming aware of the essential form with which nature is always only playing, as it were, and in playing brings forth its manifold life."

*

In April and May 1786 Goethe observed through a microscope the lower organisms that develop in infusions of different substances (banana pulp, cactus, truffles, peppercorns, tea, beer, etc.). He takes careful notes on the processes that he observes in these living entities and completes drawings of these organic forms. One can also see from these notes that Goethe does *not* seek, through such observation of lower and more simple organisms, to approach knowledge of life. It is entirely obvious that he believes he can grasp the essential traits of life processes just as well in the higher organisms as in the lower. He is of the view that in an infusorian the same kind of lawfulness repeats itself that the eye of the spirit perceives in a dog. Observation through a microscope only makes us familiar with processes that in miniature are what the unaided eye sees on a bigger scale. It provides an enrichment of sense experience. The essential being of life reveals itself to *a higher kind of seeing,* not to any tracing of sense-perceptible processes back to their smallest component parts. Goethe seeks to know this being by studying the higher plants and animals. He would without a doubt have sought this knowledge in the same way, even if the study of plant and animal anatomy had been just as far along then as it is now. If Goethe had been able to observe the cells out of which the plant and animal body builds itself up, he would have declared that in these elementary organic forms the same lawfulness is manifest that is also to be perceived in what they constitute. He would also have made sense out of the phenomena of these little entities by means of the same ideas by which he explained to himself the life processes of the higher organisms.

It is in Italy that Goethe first of all finds the thought that solves the riddle presented to him by organic forms and transformations. He leaves Karlsbad on September 3 and travels south. In few but significant sentences he describes, in his *History of My Botanical Studies,* the thought that his observation of the plant world stimulated in him up to the moment when, in Sicily, a clear mental picture revealed itself to him about how it is possible that to plant forms, "with all their self-willed, generic, and specific stubbornness, there is granted a felicitous mobility and pliancy, such that they are able to give themselves over to the many conditions that work upon them around the earth and can form and transform themselves accordingly." In his journey over the Alps, in the botanical garden in Padua, and in other places, "the changeability of plant forms" showed itself to him. "Whereas in lower-lying regions branches and stems were stronger and thicker, the buds closer to each other and the leaves broad, higher in the mountains, branches and stems became more delicate, the buds moved farther apart so that there was more space between nodes, and the leaves were more lance-shaped. I noticed this in a willow and in a gentian and convinced myself that it was not because of different species, for example. Also, near the Walchensee I noticed longer and more slender rushes than in the lowlands" *(Italian Journey,* September 8). On October 8 he finds various plants by the sea in Venice in which the interrelationship of what is organic with its environment becomes particularly visible. "They are all at the same time both thick and spare, juicy and tough, and it is obvious that the old salt in the sandy ground, but even more the salty air gives them these qualities; they are bursting with sap like water plants, and they are firm and tough like mountain plants; if the ends of their leaves have a tendency to form spines, as thistles do, then they are exceedingly sharp and strong. I found such a bush of leaves; it seemed to me to be our innocent coltsfoot, but here it was armed with sharp weapons, and the leaf was like leather, as were the seedpods and the stems also; everything was thick and fat" *(Italian Journey)*. In the botanical garden in Padua the thought takes on a particular form in Goethe's spirit as to how one might perhaps be able to develop all plant shapes out of *one* shape *(Italian Journey,* September *27);* in November he shares with Knebel: "My little bit of botany is for the first time a real pleasure to have, in these lands where a happier, less intermittent vegetation is at home. I have already made some really nice general observations whose consequences will also please you." On March *25,* 1787 he has a "good inspiration about botanical objects." He asks that Herder be informed that he will soon be ready with the archetypal plant. But he feared "that no one will want to recognize the rest of the plant world in it" *(Italian Journey).* On April 17, he goes "to the public gardens with the firm, calm intention of continuing his poetic dreaming." Only, before he is prepared for it, the being of the plants seizes him like a ghost. "The many plants, which I otherwise was used to seeing only in tubs or pots and for the greater part of the year only behind glass windows, are growing here fresh and happy in the open air, and since they can totally fulfill what they are meant to be, they become more definite and clear to us. With so many new and renewed forms in front of me, my old fancy took hold of me again: *as to whether I could not, after all, discover the archetypal plant among so great a multitude? There must after all be such a one! How would I otherwise know that this or that formation is a plant, if they were not all formed according to the same model."* He makes every effort to distinguish the varying forms, but his thoughts are always led back again to the *one* archetype that underlies them all *(Italian Journey,* April 17, 1787). Goethe begins to keep a botanical journal into which he enters all his experiences and reflections about the plant realm during his journey. The pages of this journal show how untiringly occupied he is in trying to find plant specimens that could lead him to the laws of growth and of reproduction. If he believes that he is on the track of some law or other, he sets it up first of all in a hypothetical form, in order then to let it become confirmed in the course of his further experiences. He carefully notes down the processes of germination, of fructification, of growth. It becomes more and more clear to him that the leaf is the basic organ of the plant, and that the forms of all the other plant organs can best be understood when one regards them as transformed leaves. He writes in his journal, "Hypothesis: everything is leaf, and through this simplicity the greatest manifoldness becomes possible." And on May 17 he communicates to Herder: "Furthermore I must confide to you that I am very close to discovering the secret of plant generation and organization, and that it is the simplest thing one could imagine. One can make the most beautiful observations under these skies. I have altogether clearly and beyond any doubt found where the germ is located, and that is the main point; I also already see everything else as a whole, and only a few points must still become more definite. The archetypal plant will be the most wonderful creation in the world for which nature itself will envy me. With this model and the key to it one can then go on inventing plants forever that must follow lawfully; that means: which, even if they don't exist, still could exist, and are not, for example, the shadows and illusions of painters or poets but rather have an inner truth and necessity. The same law can be applied to all other living things." "...Any way you look at it the plant is always only leaf, so inseparably joined with the future germ that one cannot think the one without the other. To grasp, to carry, to discover in nature a concept like this, is a task that puts us into a painfully sweet state" *(Italian Journey.*

In order to explain the phenomena of life Goethe takes a path that is totally different from those usually taken by natural scientists. These can be divided into two categories. There are defenders of a life force, which works in organic beings and which, with respect to other natural causes, represents a special, higher form of forces. Just as there is gravity, chemical attraction and repulsion, magnetism, etc., so also there is thought to be a life force, which brings the substances of the organism into such interaction that it can maintain itself, grow, nourish, and reproduce itself. The natural scientists who hold this view say that the same forces are working in the organism as in the rest of nature, but that they do not work as though in a lifeless machine. They are taken up, as it were, by the life force and raised to a higher level of working. Opposing the proponents of this view, there are other natural scientists who believe that there is no special life force working in organisms. They regard all manifestations of life as complicated chemical and physical processes and cherish the hope that some day they may succeed in explaining an organism like a machine by tracing it back to the effects of inorganic forces. The first view is called "vitalistic," the second one "mechanistic." Goethe's way of grasping things is totally different from both. That in the organism something else is at work besides the forces of inorganic nature seems obvious to him. He cannot adhere to the mechanistic understanding of the phenomena of life. Just as little does he seek some special life force to explain the workings of the organism. He is convinced that a different way of looking at things is needed for grasping life processes than is used in perceiving the phenomena of inorganic nature. Whoever decides to acknowledge a life force does indeed see that organic processes are not mechanical, but at the same time he lacks the ability to develop in himself that other way of looking at things by which the organic could become knowable to him. His mental picture of the life force remains dim and indefinite. A recent adherent of vitalism, Gustav Bunge, believes, "In the smallest cell, and all the riddles of life are already present in it, and in the investigation of the smallest cell, we have already reached our limits with the tools we have now" *(Vitalismus and Mechanismus,* Leipzig, 1886). It would be completely in accordance with Goethe's way of thinking to answer this in the following way. That kind of seeing that only knows the nature of inorganic phenomena has, with its tools, reached the limits that must be transcended if one is to grasp what is alive. This kind of seeing, however, will never find within its domain the means that could be capable of explaining the life of even the smallest cell. Just as the eye is needed for perception of color phenomena, so, in order to grasp life, one needs the ability to behold directly, in what is sense perceptible, something that is supersensible. This supersensible something will always escape the person who directs only his senses upon the organic forms. Goethe seeks to enliven the sense perception of plant forms in a higher way and to picture to himself the sense-perceptible form of a supersensible archetypal plant (see *The History of My Botanical Studies).* The vitalist takes refuge in his empty concept of a life force, because he simply does not see anything in an organism except what his *senses* can perceive. Goethe sees the sense-perceptible permeated by something supersensible just as a colored surface is by color.

The adherents of the mechanistic theory are of the view that we could someday succeed in creating living substances, in an artificial way, out of inorganic materials. They say that not too many years ago people maintained that there are substances in the organism that cannot arise through artificial means, but only through the working of the life force. But today, they say, one is already able artificially to create several of these substances in a laboratory. In the same way it could be possible some day, out of carbonic acid, ammonia, water, and salts, to produce a living protein, which is the basic substance of the simplest organisms. Then those of a mechanistic persuasion believe it will be irrefutably proven that life is nothing more than a combination of inorganic processes and the organism nothing more than a machine that has arisen in a natural way.

From the standpoint of the Goethean world view one would reply that the adherents of the mechanistic view speak about substances and forces in a way that is not justified by any experience. And one has become so accustomed to speak in this way that it becomes very difficult in the face of these concepts to let pure experience have its say. But let us look, without any preconceptions, at some process in the outer world. Take a quantity of water of a definite temperature. How does one know anything about this water? One looks at it and notes that it occupies space and is contained within certain limits. One sticks one's finger or a thermometer into it and finds that it has a definite degree of warmth. One touches its surface and experiences that it is fluid. Those are statements that our senses make about the state of the water. Now heat the water. It will begin to boil and finally transform itself into steam. Again one can gain knowledge for oneself about the nature of the object, the steam, into which the water has transformed itself, by perceiving it with the senses. Instead of heating the water one can apply an electric current to it under specific conditions. It transforms itself into two bodies, hydrogen and oxygen. One can also learn about the characteristics of these two bodies by what our senses tell us. One therefore perceives certain states of things in the world of objects and observes at the same time that these states pass over into other ones under certain conditions. Our senses instruct us about these states. If one speaks about something other than these states, which transform themselves, then one is no longer limiting oneself to the pure facts, but rather one is adding concepts to them as well. If one says that the oxygen and hydrogen, which an electric current has caused to arise from the water, were already contained in the water, but so intimately united with each other that they could not be perceived as they are by themselves, then one has added to one's perception a concept by which to explain to oneself how the two bodies can arise out of one body. And if one goes further and states that oxygen *(Sauerstof)* and hydrogen *(Wasserstoff)* are substances *(Stoffe),* which one does already by the names one gives them, then one has likewise added a concept to what one has perceived. For, *factually,* in the space occupied by the oxygen, there is present to perception only a certain number of states. One thinks the substance to which these states are supposed to be connected and adds it to them. What one thinks of about the oxygen and hydrogen as already present in the water, i.e., the substantial, is something thought that one adds to the content of perception. If one combines hydrogen and oxygen into water through a chemical process, then one can observe that one group of states passes over into another one. If one says that two simple substances have combined into a compound one, then one has attempted a conceptual explanation of the content of one's observation. The mental picture "substance" receives its content not from perception but rather from thinking. The same is true of "force." One sees a stone fall to earth. What is the content of that perception? A certain number of sense impressions, of states, that occur in successive places. One seeks to explain to oneself this change in the sense world and says that the earth pulls the stone. It has a "force" by which it draws the stone to itself. Again our spirit has added a mental picture to the state of affairs and has given a content to it that does not stem from perception. One does not perceive substances and forces but rather states and their transitions into one another. One *explains* these changes of state to oneself by adding concepts to the perceptions.

Imagine that there were a being who could perceive oxygen and hydrogen but not water. If we combined oxygen and hydrogen to form water before the eyes of such a being, then the states that he had perceived about the two substances would disappear before him into nothingness. If we now also described to him the states that we perceive in the water, he would not be able to picture them to himself. This proves that there is nothing in the perceptual content of oxygen from which the perceptual content water can be derived. To say that a thing consists of two or more other things means that two or more perceptual contents have changed into one unified content which, however, is a totally new one with respect to the original contents.

What would therefore be achieved if someone succeeded in artificially combining carbonic acid, ammonia, water, and salts into a living protein substance in some laboratory? One would know that the perceptual contents of many substances can combine into *one* perceptual content. But this perceptual content is absolutely not derivable from those contents. The state of living protein can only be observed in this protein itself and cannot be developed from the states of carbonic acid, ammonia, water, and salts. In the organism one has something totally different from the inorganic parts out of that it can be constructed. In the arising of a living being, sense-perceptible contents change into contents that are both sense-perceptible and supersensible. And someone who does not have the ability to make mental pictures for himself that are both sense-perceptible and supersensible can know something about the being of an organism just as little as someone would be able to experience something about water if a sense impression of it were inaccessible to him.

*

In his studies of the plant and animal worlds Goethe strove to picture to himself the organism's germination, growth, transformation of organs, nourishment, and propagation as a process both sense-perceptible and supersensible. He noted that this sensible-supersensible process in its *idea is* the same in all plants and that it takes on different forms only in its outer *manifestation*. Goethe could observe the same thing in the animal world. If one has developed in oneself the idea of the sensible-supersensible archetypal plant, then one will find it again in all individual plant forms. Diversity arises through the fact that something that is the same in idea can exist in different forms in the perceptual world. The individual organism consists of organs that can be traced back to a basic organ. The basic organ of the plant is the leaf with the node upon which it develops. In its outer manifestation this organ assumes different forms: seed leaf (cotyledon, *Keimblatt)*, leaf *(Laubblatt)*, sepal *(Kelchblatt)*, corolla "leaf" *(Kronenblatt)*, etc. "Whether the plant is sprouting, blooming, or bearing fruit, still it is always only the *same organs* which, under many different conditions and often in altered forms, are obeying the orders of nature. "In order to gain a complete picture of the archetypal plant Goethe had to follow in general the forms that the basic organ goes through in the process of a plant's growth from germination to seed maturation. At the beginning of its development, the whole plant form rests in the seed. In it the archetypal plant has taken on a shape by which it conceals its ideal content, as it were, in its outer manifestation.

> Simple was the force in the seed; a beginning model
> Lay, enclosed in itself, bent over under its husk,
> Leaf and root and germ, half-formed and without any color
> Thus the seed holds dry and protected peaceful life,
> Wells striving upward, entrusting itself to mild moistness,
> And lifts itself out of the surrounding night.

Out of the seed the plant develops its first organs, the cotyledons, after it has more or less left "its husk behind in the earth" and has established "its roots in the ground." And now shoot follows shoot in the further course of growth; node after node tower one above the other, and at every node there is a leaf. The leaves appear in different shapes. The lower ones are still simple, the upper ones variously serrated, notched, composed of several leaflets. At this stage of its development the archetypal plant spreads out its sensible-supersensible content as an outer sensible manifestation in space. Goethe pictures to himself that the leaves owe their ongoing development and refinement to the light and air. "While we find those cotyledons that are enclosed in their seed husks, to be, as it were, only stuffed with raw sap, to be not at all or only crudely organized and undeveloped, so the leaves of plants that grow under water appear to us as more crudely organized than other ones that are exposed to the open air; in fact, the same species of plant develops smoother and less refined leaves when it grows in low, moist areas, while, when transferred to higher regions, it brings forth rough, hairy leaves that are more finely developed." In the second period of growth the plant draws together again into a narrower space what it had previously spread out.

> Now it allows in less sap, it narrows its vessels,
> And the shape introduces tenderer workings thereto.
> Silent the drive of outspreading edges recedes,
> And the ribs of the stalk become more fully pronounced.
> Leafless, however, and quickly arises the tenderer stem,
> And a wondrous shape attracts the observer to it.
> Gathering around in a circle, counted and without
> Number, the smaller leaf joins with its fellow.
> Ordered round its axis, the rising chalice commits itself,
> And its highest shape in colored crowns releases.

In the calyx the plant shape draws itself together; in the corolla it spreads itself out again. Now the next contraction follows in the stamens and pistil, the organs of propagation. In the previous periods of growth the formative force of the plant developed itself in the single organs as the drive to repeat the basic form. This same force divides itself at this stage of contraction into two organs. What is thus separated seeks to find its way back together again. This occurs in the process of fructification. The male pollen present in the stamens unites itself with the female substance that is contained in the pistil; and through this the germ of a new plant is given. Goethe calls fructification a spiritual anastomosis (union) and sees in it only another form of the process that occurs in the development from one node to another. "In every body that we call living, we note the power to bring forth its own kind. When we become aware of this power in a separated form, we apply the name of the two sexes to it." From node to node the plant brings forth its own kind. For node and leaf are the simple form of the archetypal plant. In this form the bringing forth is called growth. If the force of propagation is divided into two organs then one speaks of two sexes. In this way Goethe believes he has brought the concepts of growth and procreation closer to one another. In the stage of the forming of the fruit the plant achieves its final expansion; in the seed it seems to be contracted again. In these six steps nature completes the circle of plant development and begins the whole process again from the beginning. In the seed Goethe sees only another form of the bud that develops on the leaves. The side branches that unfold from the buds are whole plants that stand upon a mother plant rather than in the earth. The mental picture of the basic organ, transforming itself in stages from seed to fruit as though upon a "spiritual ladder," is the idea of the archetypal plant. Almost as though to prove to physical vision the basic organ's ability to transform itself, nature, under certain conditions and at a particular stage, allows an organ to develop different from the one that should arise in the regular course of growth. In the double poppy, for example, at the place where stamens should arise, petals appear. The organ, that *according to the idea* was meant to be a stamen, has become a petal. In the organ, which in the normal course of plant development has a definite form, there is also contained the possibility of taking on a different form.

Goethe considers the Bryophyllum calicinum to be an illustration of his idea of the archetypal plant; this is the ordinary life plant, a species that came from the Molucca Islands to Calcutta and from there to Europe. Little new plants develop from the indentations in the plump leaves of this plant and grow into complete plants when detached. For Goethe this process shows *sense perceptibly* that in idea a whole plant lies in the leaf.

Whoever develops within himself the mental picture of the archetypal plant and keeps it so mobile that he can think it in every possible form compatible with its content can, with its help, explain for himself all the configurations of the plant realm. He will grasp the development of the individual plant, but he will also find out that all families, species, and varieties are formed in accordance with this archetypal picture. Goethe developed this view in Italy and recorded it in his book, *An Attempt to Explain the Metamorphosis of Plants,* which appeared in 1790.

*

In Italy Goethe also makes progress in developing his ideas about the human organism. On January 20 he writes to Knebel: "I am somewhat prepared for anatomy and have acquired, though not without effort, a certain level of knowledge of the human body. Here, through endless contemplation of statues, one's attention is continuously drawn to the human body, but in a higher way. The purpose of our medical and surgical anatomy is merely to know the parts, and for this a stunted muscle will also serve. But in Rome the parts mean nothing unless at the same time they present a noble and beautiful form. In the big hospital of San Spirito they have set up for artists a very beautifully muscled body in such a way that the beauty of it makes one marvel. It could really be taken for a flayed demigod, a Marsyas. It is also the custom here, following the ancients, to study the skeleton, not as an artificially arranged mass of bones but rather with the ligaments still attached from which it receives some life and movement." Even after his return from Italy Goethe industriously pursues his anatomical studies. He feels impelled to know the developmental laws of animal form in the same way that he succeeded in knowing those of the plant. He is convinced that the unity of the animal organism also rests on one basic organ that can assume various forms in outer phenomena. If the idea of the basic organ conceals itself, then the basic organ appears in an unformed way. It then manifests as the simpler organs of the animal; if the idea masters substance in such a way that it makes the substance totally into its own likeness, then the higher, nobler organs arise. That which is present in the simpler organs as idea reveals itself outwardly in the higher organs. Goethe did not succeed in drawing together the lawfulness of the entire animal form into one single mental picture as he was able to do for the plant form. He found the developmental law of one part of this form only, the spinal cord and brain, along with the bones that enclose these organs. He sees in the brain a higher development of the spinal cord. Every ganglion, every nerve center, represents for him a brain that has remained behind on a lower level. And he interprets the skull bones that enclose the brain as transformations of the vertebrae that surround the spinal cord. It has already occurred to him earlier that the posterior cranial bones (occipital, posterior, and anterior sphenoid bones) are to be regarded as three metamorphosed vertebrae; he maintains the same about the anterior cranial bones after finding on the dunes of the Lido in 1790 a sheep's skull so felicitously cracked open that the hard palate, the upper jaw bone, and the intermaxillary bone seem to present directly to his view three transformed vertebrae.

The study of animal anatomy had not yet progressed far enough in Goethe's time for him to be able to cite any creature that actually has vertebrae instead of developed cranial bones and that therefore manifests in a sense-perceptible picture what is present in the higher animals only as idea. Through the research of Carl Gegenbauer, published in 1872, it is possible to point to such an animal form. The primitive fish or selachii have cranial bones and a brain that clearly show themselves to be end parts of the spinal column and cord. According to findings about these animals, a greater number of vertebrae do seem to have gone into the head formation (at least nine) than Goethe had assumed. This error in the number of vertebrae has been brought forward against the validity of the Goethean idea of the transformation of the spinal cord and column, as has the fact that in its embryonic state the skull of the higher animals shows no trace of being composed of vertebra-like parts, but rather develops out of a simple cartilaginous sac. It is acknowledged indeed that the skull has arisen out of vertebrae. But it is denied that the cranial bones, in the form in which they manifest in the higher animals, are transformed vertebrae. It is said that a complete fusing of the vertebrae into a cartilaginous sac has occurred, in which the original vertebral structure has totally disappeared. The bone forms observable in the higher animals have then developed out of this cartilaginous capsule. These forms have not developed according to the archetype of the vertebra but rather in conformity with the tasks that they have to fulfill with the developed head. Therefore if one is seeking the explanation for one or another form of the cranial bones, one should not ask how a vertebra has metamorphosed in order to become a cranial bone but rather, what determining factors have led to the fact that this or that bone shape has separated out of the simple cartilaginous capsule? One believes in the formation of new shapes, according to new formative laws, after the original vertebral form has dissolved into a structureless capsule. Only from the standpoint of a fanaticism for facts can one find a contradiction between this view and the Goethean one. That which is no longer sense perceptible in the cartilaginous cranial capsule, i.e., the vertebral structure, is nevertheless present in it *as idea* and reappears as soon as the conditions for it are present. In the cartilaginous cranial capsule the idea of the basic organ in its vertebral form conceals itself within sense-perceptible matter; in the developed cranial bones this idea comes again into outer manifestation.

*

Goethe hopes that the laws of development of the other parts of the animal organism will reveal themselves to him in the same way as did those of the brain, spinal cord, and the parts enclosing them. About his discovery at the Lido he asks Frau von Kalb, on April 30, 1790, to tell Herder that he "has gotten one whole principle nearer to *animal form and to its manifold transformations,* and did so through the most remarkable accident." He believes himself so near his goal that in the same year that brought him his find, he wants to complete a book on animal development that could take its place beside the *Metamorphosis of the Plants* (Correspondence with Knebel). On a journey in Silesia in July 1790 he pursues his studies of comparative anatomy and begins to write an essay, *On the Form of Animals.* Goethe did not succeed in progressing from this felicitous starting point to the laws of development of the whole animal form. No matter how many attempts he makes to find the prototype of animal form, nothing analogous to the idea of the archetypal plant emerged. He compares the animals to each other and to the human being and seeks to gain *a general picture* of animal structure that nature uses as a model to form the individual shapes. This general picture of the animal prototype is not a living mental picture that fills itself with a content in accordance with the basic laws of animal development, thus recreating, as it were, the archetypal animal. It is only a general concept, which is abstracted from the particular phenomena. It ascertains what the manifold animal forms have in common;

but it does not contain the lawfulness of the animal realm.

All the parts develop according to eternal laws,
And secretly the rarest form retains the archetypal picture.
(Metamorphosis of the Animals)

Goethe could not develop a unified mental picture of how this archetypal image, by lawful transformation of one basic part, develops itself as the archetypal form, with many parts, of the animal organism. His essay, *Animal Form,* and his *Sketch of a Comparative Anatomy Proceeding from Osteology,* written in 1795 in Jena and given a more detailed shape later as *Lectures on the First Three Chapters of the Sketch of a General Introduction to Comparative Anatomy* (1796) contain only preliminary instruction as to how animals can be purposefully compared in order to gain a general picture by which the creative power "produces and develops organic beings" in order to gain a norm by which "to work out the descriptions" and to which the most varied forms can be traced "by abstracting this norm from the various animals." On the other hand Goethe showed how, with the plants, one archetypal entity develops itself lawfully through successive modifications into its complete organic shape.

*

Even though he was not able to trace nature's creative force in its forming and transforming power through the different parts of the animal organism, still Goethe did succeed in finding individual laws to which nature holds in the development of animal forms that do adhere to the general norm but that are different in their manifestations. He pictures to himself that nature does not have the ability to change the general picture at will. If nature develops and forms one part with particular completeness, this can happen only at the expense of another part. In the archetypal organism all the parts are contained that can occur in any animal. In the individual animal form one part is developed, another part is only suggested; one is particularly well elaborated, another is perhaps totally imperceptible to sense observation. In this last case Goethe is convinced that that part of the general prototype that is not *visible* in each animal is nevertheless present *as idea.*

> If you see in one creature an exceptional trait
> In some way bestowed, then ask at once where it suffers
> Elsewhere some lack, and search with investigative spirit.
> At once you will find to each form the key,
> For never did beast, with all kinds of teeth his upper
> Jaw bone bedecking, bear horns on its forehead,
> And therefore a horned lion the eternal mother
> Could not possibly fashion though she apply her full strength;
> For she has not mass enough, rows of teeth
> To fully implant and antlers and horns also to push forth.
> *(Metamorphosis of the Animals)*

In the archetypal organism all the parts are developed and maintain a balance with each other; the diversity of the individual organisms arises through the fact that the formative power expends itself on one part and therefore does not develop the outer manifestation of another part at all or only suggests it. Today one calls this law of the animal organism the law of the correlation or compensation of organs.

*

Goethe thinks the whole plant world to be contained as idea in the archetypal plant, and in the archetypal animal the whole animal world. From this thought there arises the question as to how it comes about that in one case these particular plant or animal forms arise, in another case other forms do. Under which conditions does the archetypal animal become a fish? Under which conditions a bird? The way science pictures things in order to explain the structure of organisms is repugnant to Goethe. The adherents of this way of picturing things ask with respect to each organ how it serves the living being in which it occurs. Underlying a question like this is the general thought that a divine creator or nature has prescribed a specific life's purpose for every being and has then given it a certain structure so that it can fulfill this purpose. A question like this seems just as nonsensical to Goethe as to ask what purpose a rubber ball has in moving when it is struck by another ball. An explanation of its motion can be given only by finding the laws by which the ball is set into motion by an impact or by some other cause. One does not ask what purpose the motion of the ball serves, but rather where its motion originates. In the same way, in Goethe's view, one should not ask for what purpose the bull has horns but rather *how* he can have horns. By which laws does the archetypal animal appear in the bull in a horn-bearing form? Goethe sought the idea of the archetypal plant and that of the archetypal animal in order to find in them the basis of an explanation for the diversity of organic forms. The archetypal plant is the creative element in the plant world. If one wants to explain an individual plant species, one must show how this creative element is working in a particular case. The mental picture that an organic being owes its form not to the forces working and shaping within it but rather that its form is imposed upon it from outside for certain purposes, this picture positively repels Goethe. He writes, "Recently I found, in a pitiful, apostolically monkish declamation of the Zurich prophet, the nonsensical words that *everything that has life lives by something outside itself.* Or it sounded something like that. Now a missionary can write down something like that, and when he is revising it no good spirit tugs at his sleeve" *(Italian Journey,* October 5, 1787). Goethe thinks of an organic being as a little world that is there through itself and that shapes itself according to its own laws. "The picture that a living being is brought forth for certain outer purposes and that its shape is determined by an intentional primal force to this end has already held us back in our philosophical consideration of natural things for several centuries, and still holds us back, although a few individuals have vigorously disputed this picture and shown what obstacles it lays in our path ... It is, if one may put it so, a trivial picture, which, like all trivial things, is trivial precisely because it is comfortable and sufficient for human nature as a whole." It is, of course, comfortable to say that a creator, in creating a species, has given it an underlying purposeful idea and therefore a definite shape. But Goethe wants to explain nature not by the intentions of some being located outside nature but rather by the laws of development lying within nature itself. An individual organic form arises through the fact that the archetypal plant or the archetypal animal gives itself a definite shape in a particular case. This shape must be such that the form, under the conditions in which it is living, can in fact live. "... the existence of a creature that we call fish is only possible under conditions of an element that we call water . . . " If Goethe wants to grasp what laws of development bring forth a particular organic form, he then holds on to his archetypal organism. Within it lies the power to realize itself in the most diverse outer shapes. In order to explain a fish Goethe would investigate which formative powers the archetypal animal uses in order, out of all the shapes that lie in it as idea, to bring forth specifically the fish shape. If the archetypal animal were to realize itself under certain conditions in a shape in which it cannot live, then it would perish. An organic form can *maintain* itself under certain life conditions only when it is adapted to them.

Therefore, shape determines the way of an animal's living
And this way of living works back mightily, firmly,
Upon all shapes. Thus ordered formation manifests firmly,
That to change inclines through outwardly working beings.

(Metamorphosis of the Animals)

The *enduring* organic forms in a certain life element are determined by the nature of this element. If an organic form were to come out of one life element into a different one, it would have to change itself accordingly. This can occur in particular cases, because the archetypal organism underlying the form has the ability to realize itself in countless shapes. But the transformation of the one form into the other, in Goethe's view, is not to be thought of as though outer conditions directly reshape the form in accordance with themselves but rather as though they become the stimulus by which the inner being transforms itself. Changed living conditions *stimulate* the organic form to reshape itself in a certain way according to inner laws. Outer influences work indirectly, not directly, upon the living being. Countless forms of life are contained as idea in the archetypal plant and archetypal animal; those forms come into actual existence upon which outer influences work as stimulus.

The mental picture that a species of plant or animal transforms itself into another in the course of time under certain conditions is fully justified within the Goethean view of nature. Goethe pictures to himself that the power that brings forth a new individual through the reproductive process is only a transformation of that form of power that also causes the progressive reshaping of organs in the course of growth. Reproduction is a growth above and beyond the individual. Just as the basic organ during growth undergoes successive changes, which in idea are the same, so also, in reproduction, a transformation of the outer shape can take place while holding on to the ideal archetypal picture. When an original form of an organism was present, then its descendants could change over, through gradual transformation, in the course of great periods of time, into the diverse forms that populate the earth today. The thought of an actual blood tie between all organic forms does flow out of the

basic views of Goethe. He could have expressed it right away in its complete form after conceiving his ideas of the archetypal animal and plant, but when he touches upon this thought he expresses himself hesitantly, even vaguely. One can read in the essay, *Attempt at a Theory of Comparison,* which was probably written not long after the *Metamorphosis of the Plants,* "And how worthy it is of nature that it must always employ the same means of bringing forth and nourishing a creature! Thus one will progress upon these same paths, and, just as one only at first regarded the unorganized, undetermined elements as the vehicle of the unorganized beings, so will one from now on raise one's contemplation and again regard the organized world as an interrelationship of many elements. The whole plant realm, for example, will again appear to us as an immense sea that is just as necessary for the qualified existence of the insects as the oceans and rivers are for the qualified existence of fish, and we will see that an immense number of living creatures are born and nourished in this ocean of plants; in fact, we will finally regard the whole animal world again as only one great element where one generation after another and through the other *does not arise newly* yet does maintain itself." Goethe is less reserved in the following sentence from *Lectures on the First Three Chapters of the Sketch of a General Introduction to Comparative Anatomy* (1796): "This we would therefore have gained, that we could fearlessly assert that all the more perfect organic natures—by which we mean fish, amphibians, birds, mammals, and at the peak of the latter, man—are all formed according to one archetypal picture, which more or less diverges one way or another only in its permanent parts, *and that still daily develops and transforms itself through reproduction."*
Goethe's caution about the idea of transformation is understandable. This thought was not foreign to the age in that he was developing his ideas. But this age had developed this thought in the most muddled way. "But that was a darker age,"

Goethe writes in 1807, "than one now pictures it to be. It was asserted, for example, that if the human being wanted to he could go around comfortably on all fours, and that bears could become human beings if they held themselves erect for a time. The audacious Diderot dared to suggest ways of producing goat-footed fauns to serve in uniform on the coaches of the rich and mighty, to bestow particular pomp and distinction." Goethe wanted to have nothing to do with such unclear mental pictures. He was anxious to gain an idea of the fundamental laws of the living. In this it became clear to him that the shapes of the living are not rigid and unchangeable but rather are involved in continuous transformation. Goethe did not have enough data from observation to establish in detail how this transformation occurs. It is Darwin's investigations and Haeckel's intelligent reflections that have first shed some light on the actual conditions by which individual organic forms are related. From the standpoint of the Goethean world view one can only agree with the assertions of Darwinism, insofar as they relate to the actual emerging of one organic species from another. But Goethe's ideas penetrate more deeply into the being of the organic than does the Darwinism of our day. It believes it can do without the inner driving forces in the organic that Goethe pictures to himself as a sensible-supersensible image. Yes, Darwinism even denies that Goethe was justified in speaking, from his postulates, of any *real* transformation of organs and organisms. Jul. Sachs rejects Goethe's thoughts by saying that he transfers "the abstraction that his intellect has made onto the object itself, by ascribing to the object a metamorphosis that actually has occurred only within our concept." According to this view, Goethe did nothing more than bring leaves, sepals, petals, etc. under one general concept and label them with the name "leaf." "The matter would be quite different, to be sure, if ... we could believe that in the ancestors of our present plant forms the stamens were ordinary leaves, etc." (Sachs, *History of Botany,*

1875). This view arises from the fact fanaticism that cannot see that ideas belong just as objectively to the things as what one can perceive with the senses. Goethe is of the view that one can speak of the transformation of one organ into another only if both, besides their outer manifestation, contain something else that is common to them both. This something is the sensible-supersensible form. The stamen of a present plant form can be called the transformed leaf of its ancestors only if the same sensible-supersensible form lives in both. If that is not the case, if on the present plant there simply develops a stamen at the same place where a leaf had developed on its ancestors, then nothing has transformed itself but rather one organ has taken the place of another. The zoologist Oskar Schmidt asks, "What is it then in Goethe's view that is supposed to be transformed? Definitely not the archetypal picture." *(War Goethe ein Darwinian?,* Graz, 1871). Certainly the archetypal picture does not transform itself, for it is after all the same in all forms, but precisely because it remains the same, the outer shapes can be different and still represent a unified whole. If one could not recognize the same ideal archetypal picture in two forms that have developed away from each other, then one could assume no relationship between them. Only through the mental picture of the ideal archetypal form can one connect any meaning to the assertion that organic forms arise by developing out of each other. Whoever cannot lift himself to this mental picture remains stuck in mere facts. In this mental picture lie the laws of organic development. Just as through Kepler's three basic laws the processes of the solar system are comprehensible, so through Goethe's ideal archetypal pictures are the shapes of organic nature.

*

Kant, who denies to the human spirit the ability to penetrate with ideas a totality that brings forth diversity in phenomena, calls it a "daring adventure of reason" to want to explain the individual forms of the organic world from some archetypal organism. For him, man is only able to draw together the diverse individual phenomena into a general concept, by which the intellect makes itself a picture of the unity. But this picture is only present in the human mind and has nothing to do with the creative power by which the unity really allows diversity to go forth from itself. The "daring adventure of reason" would consist of someone's assuming that the earth first releases simple organisms from her mother's womb that are less purposefully formed and that then give birth to more purposeful forms. That furthermore, still higher forms develop out of these all the way up to the most perfect living beings. If someone did make such an assumption, in Kant's opinion, he could not avoid positing an underlying purposeful creative power that gave such a push to development that all its individual members develop purposefully. Man perceives, after all, a multiplicity of diverse organisms; and since he cannot penetrate into them in order to see how they give themselves a form adapted to the life element in which they develop he must then picture to himself that they are organized from outside in such a way that they can live under these conditions. Goethe attributes to himself the ability to recognize how nature creates the individual out of the totality, the external out of the internal. He therefore wants courageously to undertake what Kant calls the "adventure of reason" (see the essay, *The Power to Judge in Beholding)*. If we had no other proof that Goethe accepted the thought of a blood relationship of all organic forms as justified within the limits indicated here, we would have to deduce it from this judgment about Kant's "adventure of reason."

*

One can guess, from Goethe's sketchy *Outline of a Morphology* that still exists that he planned to present in their successive levels the particular shapes that his archetypal plant and archetypal animal assume in the main forms of living beings. He wanted first of all to describe the being of the organic as it came to him in his reflections about animals and plants. Then, "starting at one point," to show how the archetypal organic being develops itself on the one hand into the manifold plant world, on the other hand into the multiplicity of the animal forms, how the particular forms of the worms, insects, higher animals, and the human form can be drawn forth from the common archetypal picture. Light was also meant to be shed upon physiognomy and phrenology. Goethe set himself the task of presenting the outer shape in connection with inner spiritual abilities. He felt moved to trace the organic drive to develop, that presents itself in the lower organisms in a simple outer manifestation, in its striving to realize itself stage by stage in ever more perfect shapes until in man it gives itself a form that makes him able to be the creator of spiritual productions.

This plan of Goethe's was not carried out, nor was another one that started with the fragment, *Preliminary Work for a Physiology of the Plants*. Goethe wanted to show how all the individual branches of natural science—natural history, physics, anatomy, chemistry, zoology, and physiology—must work together in order that a higher kind of contemplation may use them to explain the shapes and processes of living beings. He wanted to establish a new science, a general morphology of organisms, "not, indeed, with a new subject matter, for this is known, but rather with a new outlook and methodology; this new science would have to give a distinctive form to its findings and also indicate its place relative to other sciences . . . " The individual laws of nature provided by anatomy, natural history, physics, chemistry, zoology, and physiology should be taken up by the living mental picture of the organic and placed on a higher level, in the same way that the living being itself takes up the individual natural processes into the sphere of its development and places them on a higher level of working.

*

Goethe arrived along paths of his own at the ideas that helped him through the labyrinth of living forms. The dominant views on important areas of nature's working contradicted his general world view. He therefore had to develop mental pictures about these areas for himself that were in accordance with his nature. But he was convinced that there is nothing new under the sun and that one "could very well find indications in earlier works about what one is becoming aware of oneself." For this reason he shares his writing on the *Metamorphosis of the Plants* with learned friends and asks them to inform him whether something has already been written or handed down on this subject. He is happy when Friedrich August Wolf draws his attention to a "first-rate precursor" in Kaspar Friedrich Wolff. Goethe acquaints himself with Wolff's *Theoria Generationis,* which appeared in 1759. But one can observe, precisely with this precursor, how someone can have a correct view about the facts and still not come to the complete idea of organic development unless he is able to grasp the *sensible-supersensible form* of life, through an ability to see which is higher than that of his senses. Wolff is an excellent observer. He seeks through microscopic investigations to enlighten himself about the beginnings of life. He recognizes the calyx, corolla, stamens, pistil, and seed as transformed leaves. But he attributes the transformation to a gradual decrease in the life force, which supposedly diminishes to the same degree as the vegetation unfolds and then finally disappears entirely. Therefore calyx, corolla, etc. are for him an imperfect development of the leaves. Wolff came on the scene as an opponent of Haller, who advocated the doctrine of preformation or incapsulation. According to it all the parts of a full-grown organism were supposed to exist preformed already in miniature within the germ, and even in the same shape and interrelationship as in the complete living being. The development of an organism, consequently, is only the unfolding of what is already present. Wolff accepted as valid only what he saw with his eyes. And since, even with the most careful observations, he could not discover any incapsulated state of a living being, he regarded development as a truly new formation. The shape of an organic being is in his view not yet present in the germ. Goethe is of the same opinion with respect to outer manifestation. He also rejects the incapsulation doctrine of Haller. For Goethe the organism is in fact preformed within the germ, not as outer manifestation *but rather as idea.* He also regards the outer manifestation as a new formation. But he reproaches Wolff with the fact that where Wolff sees nothing with his physical eyes he also perceives nothing with his spiritual eyes. Wolff had no mental picture of the fact that something can still be present as idea, even if it does not come to outer manifestation. "Therefore his efforts are always to penetrate by microscopic investigations into the beginnings of life formation, and to trace in this way the organic embryos from their earliest manifestation up to full development. But no matter how excellent these methods may be, by which he has accomplished so much, still the admirable man did not think that there is a difference between seeing and seeing, that the spiritual eyes must work in continuous living alliance with the physical eyes, because one otherwise runs the danger of seeing and yet overlooking. In plant transformation he saw the same organ continuously contracting, growing smaller; but he did not see that this contraction alternated with an expansion. He saw that this organ diminished in volume, and did not notice that it ennobled itself at the same time and therefore, nonsensically, he considered atrophy to be the path to perfection."

*

To the end of his life Goethe remained in personal and written contact with numerous investigators of nature. He observed with keenest interest the progress of the science of living beings; he was happy to see how in this realm of knowledge ways of picturing things arose that approached his own ways and also how his expositions on metamorphosis were recognized and made fruitful by individual investigators. In 1817 he began to gather his works together and to publish them in a journal that he founded under the title, *On Morphology*. In spite of all this he no longer achieved through his own observation or reflection a further development of his ideas about organic development. He was only stimulated two more times to occupy himself more deeply with such ideas. In both cases his attention was caught by scientific phenomena in which he found a confirmation of his thoughts. One was the lectures that K. F. Ph. Martius held in gatherings of natural scientists in 1828 and 1829 on the *Vertical and Spiral Tendency of Vegetation* and from which the journal *Iris* published excerpts; the other one was a natural scientific dispute in the French Academy which broke out between Geoffrey de Saint-Hilaire and Cuvier in 1830.

Martius thought that the growth of plants was governed by two tendencies, by a striving in the vertical direction, which governed root and stem, and by another one that caused leaf and blossom organs, etc. to array themselves on the vertical organ in accordance with the form of a spiral line Goethe took up these ideas and brought them into connection with his mental picture of metamorphosis. He wrote a lengthy essay in which he brought together all his experiences of the plant world that seemed to him to indicate the presence of the two tendencies. He believes that he has to take up these tendencies into his idea of metamorphosis. "We had to assume that a general spiral tendency holds sway in vegetation through which, in connection with the vertical striving, every structure, every formation of plants is completed according to the law of metamorphosis." Goethe grasps the presence of spiral vessels in the individual plant organs as proof that the spiral tendency inherently rules the life of the plant. "Nothing is more in accordance with nature than the fact that what it intends as a whole it brings into activity down to the smallest detail." "In the summertime go up to a stake driven into the garden upon which a bindweed (convovulus) is climbing, winding up around it from below, and follow its lively growth with close attention. Think of the convovulus and the stake as both equally alive, rising out of one root, alternately bringing each other forth, and in this way progressing ceaselessly. Whoever can transform this sight into an inner beholding will have made this concept much easier for himself. The climbing plant seeks outside itself what it should be giving itself but cannot." Goethe uses the same comparison on March 15, 1832 in a letter to Count Sternberg and adds the words, "To be sure this comparison is not entirely apt, for at the beginning the creeper would have to wind around the rising stem in hardly noticeable circles. But the closer it came to the upper end the more quickly the spiral line would have to turn, in order finally (in the blossom) to gather together in a circle into a disk, as in dancing where quite often, when young, one was squeezed against one's will, even with the nicest children, breast to breast and heart to heart. Pardon my anthropomorphism." Ferdinand Cohn remarks about this passage, "If only Goethe could have experienced Darwin! ... how this man would have pleased him who through rigorous inductive methods knew how to find clear and convincing proofs for his ideas . . . " Darwin believes himself able to show, about almost all plant organs, that during their growth period they have the tendency to spiral-like movements, which he calls circummutation.

In September 1830 Goethe refers in an essay to the dispute between the natural scientists Cuvier and Geoffrey de Saint-Hilaire; in March 1832 he continues this essay. In February and March 1830 in the French Academy the fact fanatic Cuvier comes out against the work of Geoffrey de Saint-Hilaire, who, in Goethe's opinion, had "attained a high level of thinking in accordance with the idea." Cuvier is a master in making distinctions between the individual organic forms. Geoffrey's efforts are to seek the analogies in these forms and to furnish proof that the organization of the animals "is subject to a general plan, modified here and there, from which their differences come." He strives to know the relatedness of the laws and is convinced that the particular can gradually be developed from the whole. Goethe regards Geoffrey as a kindred spirit; he expresses this to Eckermann on August 2, 1830 in the words, "now Geoffrey de Saint-Hilaire is also definitely on our side and with him all his significant students and adherents in France.

This event is of inconceivably great value to me, and I am right to jubilate about the final victory of something to which I have dedicated my life and that is pre-eminently also my own. " Geoffrey practices a way of thinking that is also Goethe's way; in his experience of the world he seeks to grasp, along with the diversity of what is sense-perceptible, also the idea of the unity. Cuvier holds fast to the diversity, to the particular, because when he observes them the idea does not arise for him at the same time. Geoffrey has a right feeling for the relationship of the sense-perceptible to the idea; Cuvier does not have it. He therefore labels Geoffrey's comprehensive principle as presumptuous, yes, even declares it to be inferior. One can have the experience, especially with natural scientists, that they speak derogatorily about what is "merely" ideal, thought. They have no organ for what is ideal and therefore do not know the sphere of its working. Through the fact that he possessed this organ in an especially well-developed form, Goethe was led from his general world view to his deep insights into the nature of the living. His ability to let his eyes of the spirit work in a continuous living alliance with the eyes of the body enabled him to behold the unified sensible-supersensible being that extends through organic development; it enabled him to recognize this being even where one organ develops out of another, where, through transformation, an organ conceals and denies its relatedness, its sameness with the preceding one, changing both in function and form to such a degree that no comparison of outer attributes with the preceding ones can any longer take place. Seeing with the eyes of the body transmits knowledge of the sense-perceptible and material; seeing with the eyes of the spirit leads to the beholding of processes in human consciousness, to the observation of the world of thoughts, of feeling, and of will; the living alliance of spiritual and bodily eye enables one to know the organic that, as a sensible-supersensible element, lies between the purely sense-perceptible and the purely spiritual.

III

The Contemplation of the World of Colors

The Phenomena of the World of Colors

The feeling that "men's great works of art are brought forth according to *true* and *natural laws*" continuously moved Goethe to seek out these true and natural laws of artistic creation. He is convinced that the effect of a work of art must depend upon the fact that a natural lawfulness shines forth from it. He wants to know this lawfulness. He wants to know for what reason the highest works of art are at the same time the highest works of nature. It becomes clear to him that the Greeks proceeded by exactly the same laws by which nature proceeds as they "developed out of the human shape the sphere of divine formation" *(Italian Journey,* January 28, 1787). He wants to see how nature brings about this formation so that he can understand it in works of art. Goethe describes how in Italy he gradually succeeded in coming to an insight into the natural lawfulness of artistic creation (see *Confession of the Author).* "Fortunately I could hold on to a few maxims brought over from poetry and proven to me by inner feeling and long use, so that it was indeed difficult but not impossible for me, through uninterrupted looking at nature and art, through lively effective conversation with more or less insightful experts, and through continuously living with more or less practical or thinking artists, gradually to separate art in general into its parts, without fragmenting it, and to become aware of its different actively interpenetrating elements." Only one element does not want to reveal to him the natural laws by which it works in the work of art: color. Several canvases are "created and composed in his presence and carefully and thoroughly studied as to components, arrangement, and form." The artists can give him an account of how they proceed with the composition. But as soon as the topic turns to the use of color everything seems arbitrary. No one knows what relationship holds good between color and chiaroscuro and between the individual colors. Goethe cannot ascertain the basis for the fact that yellow makes a warm and comfortable impression, blue evokes a feeling of cold, that yellow and reddish-blue beside each other produce a harmonious effect. He recognizes that he must first acquaint himself with the lawfulness of the world of color *in nature,* in order from there to penetrate into the mysteries of the use of colors.

Neither the concepts about the physical nature of color phenomena that Goethe still had in his memory from student days nor the scientific compendia that he consulted for advice proved fruitful for his purpose. "Along with the rest of the world I was convinced that all the colors are contained in the light; no one had ever told me anything different, and I had never found the least cause to doubt it, because I had no further interest in this subject" *(Confession of the Author).* But as he began to be interested, he found that he could develop nothing for his purpose out of this view. The originator of this view, which Goethe found to dominate natural scientists and that still occupies the same position today, is Newton. This view asserts that white light, as it goes forth from the sun, is composed of colored lights. The colors arise through the fact that the individual component parts are separated out of white light. If one lets sunlight into a dark room through a small round opening and catches it upon a white screen set up at right angles to the direction of the in-streaming light, one obtains a white image of the sun. If one places a glass prism between the opening and the screen so that the light shines through it, the white, round sun image transforms itself. It appears shifted, drawn out lengthwise, and colored. This image is called the sun spectrum. If one holds the prism in such a way that the upper portions of the light have to take a shorter route within the volume of the glass than the lower portions do, then the colored image is shifted downward. The upper edge of the image is red, the lower edge is violet; the red goes downward into yellow, the violet upward into blue; the middle portion of the image is generally white. Only when the screen is a certain distance from the prism does the white in the middle disappear completely; the entire image appears colored, in the sequence from above downward of red, orange, yellow, green, light blue, indigo, and violet. From this experiment, Newton and his followers deduced that the colors are originally contained in the white light but mixed with one another. They are separated from each other by the prism. They have the characteristic that in passing through a transparent body they are diverted from their direction to different degrees, which means they are refracted. The red light is least, the violet is most refracted. They appear in the spectrum in the sequence of their refractibility. If one looks through the prism at a narrow strip of paper on a black background, it also appears diverted. It is both broader and colored at the edges. The upper edge appears violet, the lower red; here also the violet goes over into blue, the red into yellow; the middle is generally white. The strip of paper appears totally colored only when the prism is at a certain distance from it. Again green appears in the middle. Here also the white of the paper is supposedly divided into its colored component parts. The Newtonians have a simple explanation for the fact that all the colors appear only when the prism is at a certain distance from the screen or paper strip, whereas the middle otherwise is white. They say that the more strongly diverted lights from the upper part of the image and the more weakly diverted ones from the lower part fall together in the middle and mix into white. The colors appear only at the edges because there none of the more strongly diverted parts of the light from above can fall into the most weakly diverted parts of the light, and none of the more weakly diverted ones from below can fall into the most strongly diverted ones.

This is the view from which Goethe can develop nothing for his purposes. He therefore wants to observe the phenomena themselves. He turns to Privy Councillor Buettner in Jena who lends him the equipment with which to perform the necessary experiments. He is busy at first with other work and wants, when pressed by Buettner, to return the equipment. But before doing so he takes up a prism, in order to look through it at a completely white wall. He expects it to appear colored to different degrees. But the wall remains white. Only at those places where the white meets dark do colors arise. The window sashes appeared in the liveliest colors. From these observations Goethe believes that he can know that the Newtonian view is incorrect and that the colors are not contained in white light. The boundary, the darkness, must have something to do with the arising of colors. He continues his experiments. He looks at white surfaces upon black, and at black surfaces on a white background. He gradually forms his own view. A white disk, viewed through a prism, appears shifted. The upper portions of the disk, in Goethe's opinion, shift themselves up over the black border of the background, whereas this black background extends itself up over the lower portions of the disk. If one now looks through the prism, one sees the black background through the upper portion of the disk as though through a white veil. If one looks at the lower part of the disk, it appears through the darkness lifted up over it. Above, something light has been brought over something dark; below, something dark over something light. The upper edge appears blue, the lower one yellow. The blue goes over toward the black into violet; the yellow goes over downward into red. If the prism is moved away from the observed disk, the colored edges become broader; the blue downward, the yellow upward. When the prism is moved sufficiently far away, the yellow from below extends over the blue from above; through this overlapping green arises in the middle. To confirm this view, Goethe looks through the prism at a black disk upon a white background. Now up above something dark is brought over something light, below something light over something dark. Yellow appears above, blue below. When the edges are broadened by moving the prism away from the disk, the blue below, which goes over toward the middle into violet, is brought over the yellow above, which in broadening gradually takes on a red tone. A peach blossom color arises in the middle. Goethe said to himself that what is correct for the white disk must also hold good for the black one. "If there the light splits up into so many colors ... then here also the darkness would have to be regarded as split up into colors" *(Confession of the Author).* Goethe now relates to a physicist he knows his observations and the skepticism toward the Newtonian view that has arisen in him from them. The latter declares his skepticism to be unfounded. He explains the colored edges and the white in the middle, as well as their transition into green when the prism is moved the right distance away from the observed object, in accordance with the Newtonian view. Other natural scientists to whom Goethe brings the subject respond in the same way. He carries on by himself the observations in which he would gladly have had the help of people experienced in the field. He has a large prism made out of plate glass and fills it with pure water. Because he notices that glass prisms, whose cross section is an equilateral triangle, often hinder the observer by greatly broadening the colors that appear, he has his large prism made with the cross section of an isosceles triangle whose smallest angle is only fifteen to twenty degrees. Goethe calls those experiments *subjective* which are set up in such a way that the eye looks at an object through the prism. These experiments present themselves to the eye but are not fixed in the outer world. He wants to add objective experiments to these as well. He uses a water prism for this. The light shines through a prism and the colors are caught on a screen behind the prism. Goethe now lets sunlight go through openings cut into cardboard. He obtains thereby an illuminated space bounded on all sides by darkness. This bounded light mass goes through the prism and is deflected in its direction by it. If one holds up a screen to this light mass issuing from the prism, there arises on it an image that generally is colored on its upper and lower edges. If the prism is placed in such a way that its cross section tapers downward, then the upper edge of the image is colored blue and the lower one yellow. The blue goes over toward the dark space into violet, and toward the lighted middle into light blue; the yellow toward the darkness into red. Also in this phenomenon Goethe traces the color phenomena to the border. Above, the bright light mass streams into the dark space; it lightens something dark, which thereby appears blue. Below the dark space streams into the light mass; it darkens something light and makes it appear yellow. When the screen is moved away from the prism the colored edges become broader; the yellow approaches the blue. With the streaming of the blue into the yellow, when the screen has been moved a suitable distance from the prism, green appears in the middle of the image. Goethe makes visible to himself the streaming of the light into the dark and of the dark into the light, by shaking into the line that the light mass takes through the dark space a fine white cloud of dust that he produces with fine dry hair powder. "The more or less colored phenomenon is now caught by the white atoms and presented to the eye in its entire breadth and length" *(Color Theory,* didactic part). Goethe finds that the view that he arrived at through subjective phenomena is confirmed by objective phenomena. The colors are brought forth by the working together of light and dark. The prism serves only to shift light and dark over each other.

*

After making these experiments Goethe cannot accept the Newtonian view as his own. For him it is the same as with Haller's doctrine of incapsulation. Just as Haller thinks the fully developed organism to be already contained in the germ with all its parts, so the Newtonians believe that the colors, which under certain conditions appear with the light, are already enclosed within it. Against this belief he could use the same words that he brought against the doctrine of incapsulation, that it "rests upon a mere extrasensory fancy, upon an assumption that one believes one thinks but that can never be demonstrated in the sense world." For him the colors are new formations that are developed in connection with the light, not beings that are merely unfolded out of the light. Because of his "way of thinking in accordance with the idea" he must reject the Newtonian view. This view does not know the nature of the ideal. It acknowledges only what is factually present, what is present in the same way as the sense-perceptible. And wherever it cannot demonstrate factuality through the senses, it assumes it hypothetically. Because the colors develop in connection with the light, and must therefore already be contained in it *as idea,* this view believes that they are also factually, materially contained in the light and are only brought out by the prism and the dark border. Goethe knows that the idea is at work in the sense world; therefore he does not transfer something that is present as idea into the realm of the factual. The ideal works in inorganic nature just as in organic nature, only not as sensible-supersensible form. Its outer manifestation is completely material, merely sense-perceptible. It does not penetrate into the sense-perceptible; it does not permeate it with spirit. The processes of inorganic nature run their course in a lawful way, and this lawfulness presents itself to the observer as idea. If a person perceives white light in one place in space and colors in another place that arise in connection with the light, then a lawful relationship exists between both perceptions that can be pictured as idea. But if someone gives this idea a body and sets it out into space as something factual that passes over from the object of the one perception into that of the other perception, then that comes from his crudely physical way of picturing things. It is this crudely physical aspect about the Newtonian view that repelled Goethe. It is the idea that leads one inorganic process over into the other, not something factual that travels from one to the other.

The Goethean world view can acknowledge only two sources for all knowledge of the inorganic nature processes: that which is sense-perceptible about these processes, and the *ideal* interconnections of the sense-perceptible that reveal themselves to thinking. The ideal interconnections within the sense world are not of the same kind. There are some that are directly obvious when sense perceptions appear beside each other or after each other, and others that one can see only when one traces them back to some of the first kind. In the manifestation that offers itself to the eye when it looks at something dark through something light and perceives blue, Goethe believes he recognizes an interconnection of the first kind between light, darkness, and color. It is the same thing when something light looked at through something dark gives yellow. The spectrum that appears at the borders allows us to recognize an interconnection that becomes clear to immediate observation. The spectrum that manifests in a sequence of seven colors from red to violet can only be understood when one sees how other determining factors are added to those through which the border phenomena arise. The simple border phenomena have joined in the spectrum into a complicated phenomenon that can be understood only when one traces it back to the basic phenomena. That which stands before the observer in its purity in the basic phenomenon appears impure, modified in that that is complicated by the additional determining factors. The simple facts are no longer directly recognizable. Goethe therefore seeks everywhere to trace complicated phenomena back to simple pure ones. He sees the explanation of inorganic nature to consist of this leading back. He goes no further than the pure phenomenon. In it an ideal interconnection of sense perceptions reveals itself that explains itself through itself. Goethe calls the pure phenomenon "archetypal phenomenon" *(Urphaenomen).* He regards it as idle speculation to reflect further upon the archetypal phenomenon. "The magnet is an archetypal phenomenon that one only has to state in order to have explained it" *(Aphorisms in Prose).* A composite phenomenon is explained when one shows how it is built up out of archetypal phenomena. Modern science proceeds differently from Goethe. It wants to trace the processes in the sense world back to the movements of the smallest particles of the body and, to explain these movements, uses the same laws by which it comprehends the movements that occur visibly in space. To explain these visible movements is the task of mechanics. If the movement of a body is observed then mechanics asks by which force it was set in motion; what distance it travels in a particular time; what form the line has in which it moves; etc. It seeks to represent mathematically the interrelationships of force, of the distance traveled, of the form of the path. Now the scientist states that the red light can be traced back to the oscillating movement of the body's smallest particles that spreads itself out in space. This movement is comprehended by applying to it the laws won through mechanics. The science of inorganic nature considers its goal to be gradually to go over entirely into *applied mechanics.*

*

Modern physics asks about the number of vibrations in a time unit that correspond to a particular color quality. From the number of vibrations that correspond to red, and from those that correspond to violet, it seeks to determine the physical relationship of both colors. The qualitative disappears from its view; it looks at the spatial and temporal aspects of the processes. Goethe asks what relation exists between red and violet when one disregards the spatial and temporal and looks merely at the qualitative aspect of the colors. A postulate of the Goethean way of looking at things is that the qualitative is also really present in the outer world and forms one inseparable whole with the temporal and spatial. Modern physics on the other hand must start with the basic view that only the quantitative, only lightless and colorless processes of movement are present in the outer world, and that everything qualitative arises only as the effect of the quantitative upon the sense- and spirit-endowed organism. If this assumption were correct, then the lawful interrelationships of the qualitative could also not be sought in that outer world but would have to be traced back to the nature of the sense organs, of the nervous system, and of the organ of mental picturing. The qualitative elements of processes would then not be for physics to investigate but rather for physiology and psychology. Modern science does proceed in accordance with this presupposition. In its view the organism, in a way appropriate to the constitution of its eyes, optic nerve, and brain, translates one process of movement into the sensation red and another into the sensation violet. Therefore all the outer aspects of the color world are explained when one has seen the interconnection of the processes of movement by which this world is determined.

A proof for this view is sought in the following observation. The optic nerve senses every outer impression as a light sensation. Not only light but also a bump or pressure on the eye, a tug on the retina when the eye is moved quickly, an electric current conducted through the head: all these also cause a sensation of light. A different sense experiences the same things in a different way. Bumps, pressure, tugs, electrical current, when they stimulate the skin, cause sensations of touch. Electricity stimulates in the ear a sound sensation, in the tongue a taste sensation. One deduces from this that the content of sensation, which arises in the organism through an outer effect, is different from the outer process by which it is caused. The red color is not experienced by the organism because the color is connected with a corresponding process of movement outside in space but rather because the eye, optic nerve, and brain of the organism are constituted in such a way that they translate a colorless process of movement into a color. The law expressed in this way was called the law of specific sense energies by the physiologist Johannes Mueller who first established it.

This observation proves only that the sense- and spirit-endowed organism can translate impressions of the most diverse kinds into the language of the senses upon which they act, but not that the content of every sense impression is also present only inside the organism. When the optic nerve is tugged there arises an indefinite, completely general stimulation that contains nothing that would cause one to place its content out in space. A sensation that arises through a real light impression is inseparably connected in its content with the spatial-temporal that corresponds to it. The movement of a body and its color are content of perception in exactly the same way. If one pictures the movement in and for itself, one is abstracting from what is otherwise perceived about the body. All the other mechanical and mathematical mental pictures are taken from the world of perception in the same way as movement. Mathematics and mechanics arise through the fact that one part is separated out from the content of the world of perception and considered in and for itself. Within reality there are no objects or processes whose content is exhausted when one has grasped about them what can be expressed through mathematics and mechanics. Everything mathematical and mechanical is connected to color, warmth, and other qualities. If it is necessary for physics to assume that for the perception of a color there are corresponding vibrations in space, of which a very small expansion and a very great velocity are characteristic, then these movements can only be thought of as analogous to the movements that occur visibly in space. That means, if the world of objects is thought of as in movement, right into its smallest elements, then it must also be pictured as being endowed, right into its smallest elements, with color, warmth, and other characteristics. Whoever takes colors, warmth, sounds, etc. to be qualities that exist as effects of outer processes through the mentally picturing organism and that exist only inside this organism, must also transfer into it everything mathematical and mechanical that is connected with these qualities. Then, however, nothing more is left him for his outer world. The red that I see and the light vibrations that the physicist demonstrates as corresponding to this red are in reality a unity that only the abstracting intellect can separate from one another. I would see the vibrations in space, which correspond to the quality "red," as movement, if my eye were organized to do so. But I would have connected with the movement, the impression of the red color.

Modern natural science transfers out into space an unreal abstraction, a vibrating substratum stripped of all qualities of sensation, and is astonished then that one cannot understand what can cause the mentally picturing organism, endowed with nerve apparatus and brain, to translate these indifferent processes of motion into the colorful sense world filled with warmth differentiations and sounds. Du Bois-Reymond therefore assumes that man, because of an insurmountable limit to his knowing, will never understand how the fact that "I taste sweetness, smell the fragrance of roses, hear organ tones, see red" is connected with certain movements of the smallest bodily particles in the brain, whose movements are in turn caused by the vibrations of the tasteless, odorless, soundless, and colorless elements of the outer world of objects. "It is indeed thoroughly and forever incomprehensible that it should not be a matter of indifference to a number of atoms of carbon, hydrogen, nitrogen, oxygen, etc. how they lie and move, how they lay and moved, how they will lie and move" *(Limits to Knowing Nature,* Leipzig, 1882). But there are absolutely no limits to knowledge here. Wherever in space there are a number of atoms in a definite movement, there is necessarily a definite quality (red, for example) also present. And conversely, where red appears movement must be present. Only a thinking that abstracts can separate the one from the other. Whoever thinks of the movement as separated within reality from the other content of the process to which the movement belongs cannot find the transition again from the one to the other.

Only that about a process that is movement can be traced back again to movement; that which belongs to the qualitative element of the world of colors and light can also be traced back only to a similar qualitative element within the same realm. Mechanics traces complex movements back to simple ones that are immediately comprehensible. Color theory must trace complicated color phenomena back to simple ones that can be recognized in the same way. A simple process of movement is an archetypal phenomenon just like the emergence of yellow out of the interworking of light and dark. Goethe knows what the mechanical archetypal phenomena can accomplish for the explanation of inorganic nature. Whatever is not mechanical within the world of objects he leads back to archetypal phenomena that are not of a mechanical kind. Goethe has been reproached for having thrown out the mechanical way of looking at nature and for limiting himself only to the observation and stringing together of the sense-perceptible (see Harnack, for example, in his book, *Goethe in the Period of his Completeness).* Du Bois-Reymond finds *(Goethe and More Goethe,* Leipzig, 1883) that "Goethe's theorizing limits itself to allowing other phenomena to emerge from an archetypal phenomenon, as he calls it, in somewhat the way fog assumes successive shapes without any intelligible causal connection. *It was the concept of mechanical causality that was totally lacking in Goethe."* But what else does mechanics do than let complex processes go forth out of simple archetypal phenomena? Goethe did exactly the same thing in the sphere of the color world that the physicist accomplishes in the sphere of processes of motion. Because Goethe is not of the view that all processes in inorganic nature are purely mechanical, it has therefore been denied that he has any concept of mechanical causality. Whoever does this only shows that he is himself in error as to what mechanical causality signifies within the world of objects. Goethe remains in what is qualitative about the world of light and colors; he leaves it up to others to express the quantitative, mechanical, mathematical. He "sought to keep his theory of color absolutely at a distance from mathematics, although right away certain points manifest clearly enough where the help of the art of measurement would be desirable ... But this lack may even be of benefit, inasmuch as it can now become the business of the ingenious mathematician himself to seek out where color theory needs his help, and how he can make his contribution to the perfecting of this part of natural philosophy" (Paragraph 727 of the didactic part of the *Color Theory).* The qualitative elements of the sense of sight, light, darkness, colors, must first be understood out of their own interconnections, be traced back to archetypal phenomena; then there can be investigated on a higher level of thinking what the relationship is between these interconnections and the quantitative, the mechanical-mathematical elements in the world of light and colors. Goethe wants to trace the connections within the qualitative realm of the color world back to the simplest elements in just as strict a sense as the mathematician or the mechanic does in his sphere. "We must learn from the mathematicians to take care to place next to each other only the elements that are closest to each other, or rather to deduce from each other the elements that are closest to them, and even where we use no calculations, we must always proceed as though we *were obliged to render account to the strictest geometrician.* For actually it is the mathematical method that, because of its carefulness and purity, reveals right away any jump in its assertions, and its proofs are actually only detailed expositions showing that what is presented in combination was already there in its simple components and in its whole sequence, was viewed in its full scope and was correctly and irrefutably devised under all conditions" *(The Experiment as Mediator between Subject and Object).*

*

Goethe draws the principles of explanation for phenomena directly from the realm of observation. He shows how the phenomena are interconnected *within* the experienceable world. For grasping nature he rejects mental pictures that point outside the region of observation. Any kind of explanation that oversteps the field of experience by bringing in factors to explain nature that by their very nature are not observable contradicts the Goethean world view. Just such an explanation is the one that seeks the nature of light in a light substance that as such is not perceived itself but that can only be observed as light in its way of working. Among this kind of explanation is the one that reigns in modern natural science, according to which the processes of movement of the world of light are carried out, not by the perceptible qualities that are given to the sense of sight, but rather by the smallest particles of imperceptible matter. It is not contrary to the Goethean world view to picture to oneself that a particular color is connected to a particular process of movement in space. But it is altogether contrary to it to maintain that this process of movement belongs to some realm of reality located outside of experience, belongs to the world of matter that can, indeed, be observed in its effects, but not in its own being. For one who adheres to the Goethean world view the vibrations of light in space are processes that should not be accorded a kind of reality different from the rest of the content of perception. They elude direct observation not because they lie beyond the realm of experience but rather because human sense organs are not so finely organized that they directly perceive movements of such minuteness. If an eye were organized in such a way that it could observe in every detail the vibration of a thing that repeats itself four hundred billion times in one second, then such a process would present itself in exactly the same way as a process in the crudely perceptible world. That means, the vibrating thing would manifest the same characteristics as other things of perception.

Every kind of explanation that traces the things and processes of experience back to other ones not located within the field of experience can attain content-filled mental pictures about this region of reality lying beyond observation only by borrowing certain characteristics from the world of experience and carrying them over onto the unexperienceable. In this way the physicist carries over hardness, impenetrability, onto the smallest elements of bodies, to which he still further ascribes the ability to attract and repel their own kind; on the other hand he does not attribute color, warmth, and other characteristics to these elements. He believes he explains an experienceable process of nature by leading it back to one that is not experienceable. According to Du Bois-Reymond's view, to know nature is to lead the processes in the world of objects back to the movements of atoms that are caused by their attracting and repelling forces *(Limits to Knowing Nature,* Leipzig, 1882). Matter, the substance filling space, is considered to be what is moving in all this. This substance is supposed to have been there from all eternity and will be there for all eternity. But matter is not supposed to belong to the sphere of observation but rather to be present beyond it. Du Bois-Reymond therefore assumes that man is incapable of knowing the real nature of matter itself, that he therefore leads the processes of the world of objects back to something whose nature will remain forever unknown to him. "We will never know better than we know today what haunts the space here where matter is" *(Limits to Knowing Nature).* When considered more exactly this concept of matter dissolves into nothing. The real content that one gives to this concept is borrowed from the world of experience. One perceives movements within the world of experience. One feels a pull when one holds a weight in one's hand, and a pressure when one lays a weight upon the palm of one's hand held out horizontally. In order to explain this perception one forms the concept of force. One pictures to oneself that the earth draws the weight to itself. The force itself cannot be perceived. It is ideal. But it belongs nevertheless to the sphere of observation. The mind observes it, because the mind sees the ideal relationships of the perceptions to one another. One is led to the concept of a force of repulsion when squeezing a piece of rubber and then letting it go. It restores itself to its previous shape and size. One pictures to oneself that the compressed parts of the rubber repel each other and again occupy their previous space. The way of thinking now under consideration carries such mental pictures, derived from observation, into an unexperienceable sphere of reality. It therefore in reality does nothing more than to trace something experienceable back to another experienceable something. Only, it arbitrarily shifts the latter into the sphere of the unexperienceable. It can be shown, of any way of picturing things that speaks of something unexperienceable within its view of nature, that it takes up a few scraps from the sphere of experience and relegates them to a sphere of reality located beyond observation. If one takes the scraps of experience out of the mental picture of the unexperienceable, there then remains a concept without content, a non-concept. The explanation of something experienceable can only consist of one's leading it back to something else that is experienceable. One finally arrives at elements within experience that can no longer be traced back to other ones. These are not further explainable, because they need no explanation. They contain their explanation in themselves. Their immediate being consists of what they present to observation. For Goethe, light is such an element. According to his view, a person has come to know the light who without preconception perceives light in its manifestation. The colors arise in connection with light and their arising is understood when one shows *how* they arise in connection with light. Light itself is given in direct perception. One knows what is ideally inherent in it when one observes what connection there is between it and the colors. From the standpoint of the Goethean world view it is impossible to ask about the real nature of light, about something unexperienceable that corresponds to the phenomenon "light." "For actually it is a vain undertaking to express the real nature of a thing. We become aware of workings, and a complete history of these workings would very well comprise, if need be, the real nature of that thing." This means that a complete presentation of the workings of something experienceable comprises all the manifestations that are *inherent* in it *as idea.* "We struggle to no avail to portray the character of a person; but put together his actions, his deeds, and a picture of his character will come to meet us. The colors are deeds of the light, deeds and sufferings *(Leiden)."* In this sense we can expect from them disclosures about the light" (didactic part of the *Color Theory,* Preface).

Light presents itself to observation as "the simplest, most undivided, most homogeneous being that we know" (Correspondence with Jacobi). Confronting it is the darkness. For Goethe darkness is not the completely powerless absence of light. It is something active. It confronts the light and enters with it into a mutual interaction. Modern natural science sees darkness as a complete nothingness. According to this view, the light that streams into a dark space has no resistance from the darkness to overcome. Goethe pictures to himself that light and darkness relate to each other like the north and south pole of a magnet. The darkness can weaken the light in its working power. Conversely, the light can limit the energy of the darkness. In both cases color arises. A view in physics that thinks of darkness as that which is completely inactive cannot speak of any such interaction. It must therefore trace the colors back to light alone. Darkness arises for observation as a phenomenon just as much as light does. What is dark is content of perception in the same sense as what is light. The one is only the opposite of the other. The eye that looks out into the night mediates the real perception of darkness. Were the darkness an absolute nothingness, then no perception at all would arise when the human being looks out into the dark.

Yellow is a light that has been dampened by the darkness; *blue is* a darkness that has been weakened by the light.

*

The eye is organized to mediate to the mentally picturing organism the phenomena of the world of light and color and the interconnections of these phenomena. In this it does not conduct itself in a merely receptive way but rather enters into a lively interaction with the phenomena. Goethe's striving is to know the nature of this interaction. He regards the eye as something altogether living and wants to gain insight into what its life manifests. How does the eye relate itself to the individual phenomenon? How does it relate itself to the interconnections of the phenomena? Those are questions that he poses himself. Light and darkness, yellow and blue are opposites. How does the eye experience these opposites? It must lie in the nature of the eye that it also experiences the interrelationships that exist between the individual perceptions. For, "the eye has the light to thank for its existence. Out of indifferent animal auxiliary organs, the light calls forth an organ for itself of its own kind; and thus the eye forms itself in connection with the light for the light, so that the inner light can come to meet the outer light" (didactic part of the *Color Theory,* Introduction).

Just as light and darkness act in opposition to each other in outer nature, so are the two states, into which the eye is brought by the two phenomena, opposite to each other. When one keeps one's eye open in a dark space, a certain lack makes itself felt. If on the other hand the eye is turned toward a brightly illuminated white surface, it becomes unable for a time to distinguish moderately illuminated objects. Seeing into the dark increases receptivity; seeing into brightness weakens it.

Every impression upon the eye remains for a time within it. Whoever looks at the black cross-pieces between window panes against a bright background will, when he closes his eyes, still have the phenomenon before him for a while. If, while the impression still lasts, one looks at a light gray surface, the cross appears bright, the panes, on the other hand, dark. A reversal of the phenomenon occurs. It follows from this that the eye is predisposed through the one impression to create out of itself the opposite one. Just as in the outer world light and darkness stand in a relationship with each other, so also do the corresponding states in the eye. Goethe pictures to himself that the place in the eye upon which the dark cross fell is rested and receptive to a new impression. Therefore the gray surface works upon it in a livelier way than upon the other places in the eye that previously have received the stronger light from the window panes. The bright produces in the eye an inclination to the dark, the dark an inclination to the bright. If one holds a dark image in front of a light gray surface and, when the image is taken away, looks fixedly upon the same spot, the space that the dark image occupied appears much lighter than the rest of the surface. A gray image against a dark background appears brighter than the same image does against a light background. The eye is predisposed by the dark background to see the image as brighter, but the light background as darker. Through these phenomena there is indicated to Goethe the great activity of the eye "and the quiet opposition that every living thing is driven to show when any particular state is presented it. Thus, breathing in already presupposes breathing out, and vice versa ... It is the eternal formula of life that manifests itself here also. When the eye is offered the dark, it then demands the bright; it demands dark when one confronts it with bright and precisely through this shows its liveliness, its right to grasp the object by bringing forth from itself something that opposes the object" (Para. 38 of the didactic part of the *Color Theory).*

In the same way as light and darkness, color perceptions also call forth a counter activity in the eye. Hold a small piece of yellow paper in front of a moderately illuminated white screen and look fixedly at the small yellow surface. After a while take the paper away. At the place that the paper filled, one will see violet. The eye is predisposed by the impression of the yellow to produce the violet out of itself. In the same way blue will bring forth orange, and red green as a counter activity. Every color sensation therefore has a living connection in the eye with another. The states into which the eye is brought by perceptions stand in a relationship similar to that of the contents of these perceptions in the outer world.

*

When light and darkness, bright and dark, work upon the eye, then this living organ comes to meet them with its demands; when they work upon things outside in space, then the things enter into interaction with them. Empty space has the characteristic of transparency. It does not at all affect light and darkness. These shine through it in their own lively nature. The case is different when space is filled with things. This filling of space can be such that the eye does not become aware of it because light and darkness in their original form shine right through it. Then one speaks of transparent things. If light and darkness do not shine unweakened through a thing, then it is called *turbid.* A turbid filling of space offers the possibility of observing light and darkness, bright and dark in their mutual relationship. Something bright, seen through something turbid, appears yellow; something dark, seen through something turbid, appears blue. What is turbid is something material that has been brightened by light. Against a brighter livelier light located behind it, what is turbid is dark; against a darkness that shines through it, it acts like something bright. Therefore, when something turbid confronts the light or darkness, there really work into one another an existing brightness and an existing dark.

If the turbidity, through which the light is shining, gradually increases, then the yellow passes over into yellowish red and then into ruby red. If the turbidity, through that the dark is penetrating, lessens, then the blue goes over into indigo and finally into violet. Yellow and blue are basic colors. They arise through the working together of brightness or dark with turbidity. Both can take on a reddish tone, the former through an increasing of the turbidity, the latter by a lessening of it. Red, accordingly, is not a basic color. It appears as a color tone connected to yellow or blue. Yellow, with its reddish nuances that intensify as far as pure red, is close to the light; blue, with its shades, is related to the darkness. When blue and yellow mix, green arises; if blue that has been intensified to violet mixes with yellow that has been darkened into red, then the purple color arises.

Goethe pursues these basic phenomena within nature. The bright disk of the sun, seen through a haze of turbid vapors, appears yellow. Dark cosmic space, viewed through the vapors of the atmosphere that are illumined by the light of day, presents itself as the blue of the heavens. "In the same way the mountains also appear blue to us: for, through our viewing them at such a distance that we no longer see their local colors, and that light from their surfaces no longer works upon our eye, they act as a pure dark object that now appears blue through the vapors between them and us" (Para. 156 of the didactic part of the *Color Theory).*

Out of his absorption in the works of painters the need grew in Goethe to penetrate into the laws to which the phenomena of the sense of sight are subject. Every painting presented him with riddles. How does chiaroscuro relate to the colors? In what relationships do the individual colors stand to one another?

Why does yellow give a happy mood, blue a serious one? Out of the Newtonian theory of color there was no way of gaining a viewpoint from which these mysteries could be revealed. This view traces all colors back to light, arranges them sequentially side by side, and says nothing about their relationships to the dark, and also nothing about their living connections to each other. From insights gained along his own path, Goethe was able to solve the riddles that art had posed him. Yellow must possess a happy, cheerful, mildly stimulating character, for it is the color closest to light. It arises through the slightest toning down of the light. Blue points to the dark that works in it. Therefore it gives a feeling of cold just as "it also reminds one of shadows." Reddish yellow arises through the intensification of yellow toward the dark pole. Through this intensification its energy grows. The happy, cheerful feeling passes over into the blissful. As soon as the intensification goes still further, from reddish yellow into yellowish red, the happy, blissful feeling transforms itself into the impression of something forceful. Violet is blue that is striving toward the bright. Through this the restfulness and cold of blue become restlessness. In bluish red this restlessness experiences a further increase. Pure red stands in the middle between yellowish red and bluish red. The storminess of the yellow appears lessened, the languid restfulness of the blue enlivens itself. The red gives the impression of ideal contentment, of the equalizing of opposites. A feeling of contentment also arises through green, that is a mixture of yellow and blue. But because here the cheerfulness of the yellow is not intensified, and the restfulness of the blue is not disturbed by a reddish tone, the contentment will be a purer one than that which red brings forth.

*

When a color is brought to it, the eye right away asks for another one. When it looks at yellow, there arises in it the longing for violet; when it perceives blue, it then demands orange;

when it sees red, it then desires green. It is comprehensible that the feeling of contentment arises when, beside a color that is presented to the eye, another one is placed for which, in accordance with its nature, it is striving. The law of color harmony results from the nature of the eye. Colors that the eye asks for side by side have a harmonious effect. If two colors appear side by side that do not ask for each other, then the eye is stimulated to react. The juxtaposition of yellow and purple has something one-sided, but happy and magnificent. The eye wants violet next to yellow in order to be able to live in accordance with its nature. If purple takes the place of violet then the object asserts its claims over against those of the eye. It does not accomodate itself to the demands of this organ. Juxtapositions of this kind serve to indicate what is *significant* about the things. They do not want unconditionally to satisfy but rather to characterize. Those colors lend themselves to such characteristic connections that do not stand in complete opposition to each other but that also do not go directly over into each other. Juxtapositions of this latter kind give something characterless to the things on which they occur.

*

The becoming and being of the phenomena of light and colors revealed itself to Goethe in nature. He also recognized it again in the creations of the painters in which it is raised to a higher level, is translated into the spiritual. Through his observations of the perceptions of sight Goethe gained a deep insight into the relationship of nature and art. He must have been thinking of this when, after the completion of the *Color Theory,* he wrote to Frau von Stein about these observations: "I do not regret having sacrificed so much time to them. Through them I have attained a culture that would have been difficult for me to acquire from any other side."

The Goethean color theory differs from that of Newton and of those physicists who construct their views upon Newton's mental pictures, because Goethe takes his start from a world view different from that of these physicists. Someone who does not really see the connection described here between Goethe's general picture of nature and his theory of color cannot do anything other than believe that Goethe came to his views on color because he lacked a sense for the physicist's genuine methods of observation. Someone with insight into this connection will also see that within the Goethean world view no other theory of color is possible than his. He would not have been able to think differently about the nature of color phenomena than he did, even if all the discoveries made since his time had been spread out before him, and if he himself could have employed with exactness the modern experimental methods that have become so refined. Even if, after becoming aware of the discovery of the Frauenhofer lines, he cannot fully incorporate them into his view of nature, neither they nor any other discovery in the realm of optics contradict his conception. The point in all this is only to build up this Goethean conception in such a way that these phenomena fit themselves into this conception. Admittedly, someone who stands on the point of view of the Newtonian conception would not be able to picture to himself anything of Goethe's views on colors. But this does not stem from the fact that such a physicist knows of phenomena that contradict the Goethean conception but rather from the fact that he has accustomed himself to a view of nature that hinders him from knowing what the Goethean view of nature actually wants.

IV

Thoughts about the Developmental History of the Phenomena of Earth and Air

Thoughts about the Developmental History of the Earth

Through his involvement with the Ilmenau mine Goethe was stimulated to study the realm of the minerals, rocks, and types of stone, as well as the superimposed strata of the earth's crust. In July 1776 he accompanies Duke Karl August to Ilmenau. They wanted to see whether the old mine could be started up again. Goethe also devoted further care to this matter. Through this there grew in him more and more the urge to know how nature goes about the formation of its great stone masses and mountains. He climbed high peaks and crept into the depths of the earth in order "to discover the most immediate traces of the great shaping hand." On September 8, 1780 from Ilmenau he shared with Frau von Stein his joy at learning to know creative nature also from this side. "I am living now body and soul in stone and mountains, and am very happy about the broad perspectives that are opening up to me. These last two days have conquered a large area for me and can suggest a great deal. The world is taking on for me now a new and vast appearance." More and more the hope takes hold in him that he will succeed in spinning a thread that can guide him through the underground labyrinth and give him an overview in the confusion (letter to Frau von Stein on June 12, 1784). Gradually he extends his observations over other regions of the earth's surface. On his journeys in the Harz Mountains he believes he recognizes how great inorganic masses take shape. He ascribes to them the tendency "to divide in manifold regular directions in such a way that parallelepipeds arise that in turn are inclined to split diagonally." (See the essay, "The Shaping of Large Inorganic Masses.") He thinks of stone masses as interpenetrated by an ideal latticework, and this in a six-sided way. Through this, cubic, parallelepipedic, rhombic, rhomboidal, pillar, and plate-shaped bodies are cut out of a basic mass. He pictures to himself within this basic mass forces at work that divide it in the way that the ideal lattice-work makes visible. As in organic nature, so Goethe also seeks in the stone realm for the idea at work in it. Here also he investigates with spiritual eyes. Where the division into regular forms does not come to appearance, he assumes that it is present as idea in the masses. On a journey in the Harz Mountains that he undertakes in 1784, he asks Councillor Kraus, who is accompanying him, to execute pastel drawings in which the invisible, ideal is made clear by the visible and brought to view. He believes that what is actually present can be truly portrayed by the painter only when he is attentive to the intentions of nature that often do not emerge clearly enough in the outer phenomenon. "... in the transition from the soft into the rigid state, a separation results, which either applies now to the whole, or that occurs in the most inward part of the masses" (Essay on "Formation of Mountains as a Whole and in its Farts"). In Goethe's view a sensible-supersensible archetypal picture is livingly present in organic forms; something ideal enters into the sense perception and permeates it. In the regular formation of inorganic masses there works something ideal that as such does not enter into the sense-perceptible form taut that does nevertheless create a sense-perceptible form. The inorganic form is not sensible-supersensible in its manifestation but only sense-perceptible; but it must be considered to be an effect of a supersensible force. It is an intermediate thing between the inorganic *process* whose course is still governed by something ideal but that receives a finished form from this ideal, and the organic in which the ideal itself becomes sense-perceptible form.

Goethe thinks the formation of composite rocks to have been caused by the fact that the substances that were originally present in a mass only as idea are then actually separated out of each other. In a letter to Leonhard on November 25, 1807, he writes, "I gladly admit that I still often see simultaneous operations where other people see a successive operation; that, in many a rock that others consider to be a conglomerate, a rock brought together out of fragments and fused together, I believe I see something differentiated and separated out of a heterogeneous mass and then held rigidly together by consolidation..."

Goethe did not reach the point of making these thoughts fruitful for a larger number of inorganic developments of form. It is in accordance with his way of thinking to explain even the ordering of geological strata by ideal formative principles that are inherent in substance by its very nature. He could not adhere to the then widespread geological views of Werner, because Werner did not know such formative principles but rather traced everything back to the purely *mechanical* action of water. Even more repugnant to him was the Volcanism that Hutton had presented and that Alexander von Humboldt, Leopold von Buch, and others defended, which explained the development of the various periods of the earth by mighty revolutions, brought about by material causes. This view lets great mountain systems shoot suddenly forth from the earth by volcanic forces. Such enormous *tours de force* seem to Goethe to contradict the being of nature. He saw no reason that the laws of earth development should suddenly change at certain times and, after long, ongoing, and *gradual* activity, should manifest at a certain point in time as "heaving and shoving, thrusting up and crushing, hurling and smashing." Nature seemed to him to be consistent in all its parts, so that even a god could change nothing about its inborn laws. He considers its laws to be unchangeable. The forces at work today in the formation of the earth's surface must by their very being have worked in all ages.

From this viewpoint he also arrives at a view, in accordance with nature, as to how the blocks of stone that are to be found strewn about near the Lake of Geneva and that, to judge by their composition, were separated from far-away mountains, got there. He was confronted by the opinion that these rock masses were hurled there by the tumultuous eruption of mountains located far inland. Goethe sought forces that can be observed today and that are able to explain this phenomenon. He found such forces active in the formation of glaciers. He needed only to assume now that the glaciers that today still bring rock from mountains into the plains once had an immensely greater scope than at present. They then carried the rock masses much farther away from the mountains than they do in the present day. As the glaciers receded again, these rocks were left behind. Goethe thought that the granite boulders that lie about in the low plains of northern Germany must also have arrived at their present location in an analogous way. In order to be able to picture to oneself that the areas that are erratically strewn with boulders were once covered by glacial ice, one needs to assume an age of great cold. This assumption became the common property of science through Agassiz, who came to it independently and in 1837 presented it in the Swiss Society for Natural Scientific Research. In recent times this age of cold, which broke in upon the continents of the earth when a rich animal and plant life was already developed, has become the favorite study of eminent geologists. The details that Goethe brings forward about the phenomena of this "ice age" are unimportant in the face of observations made by later researchers.

Just as in his assumption of an age of great cold, Goethe is led by his general view of nature to a correct view about the nature of fossils. It is true that earlier thinkers had already recognized these entities as the remains of organisms from former ages. But this view was so long in becoming the generally dominant one that Voltaire could still consider fossilized mussels to be freaks of nature. After gaining some experience in this area

Goethe soon recognized that the fossils, as remains of organisms, stand in a natural relationship to those earth strata in which they are found. That means that these organisms lived during those epochs of the earth in which the corresponding strata were formed. He expresses himself in this way about fossils in a letter to Merck on October 27, 1782: "All the remains of bones of which you speak and that are found everywhere in the upper level of the earth, stem, I am fully convinced, from the most recent epoch that, however, compared to our usual reckoning of time, is immensely old. In this epoch the sea had already receded; on the other hand rivers still flowed, of great breadth, yet relating to the level of the sea, not faster than now and perhaps not even as fast. At the same time, the sand, mixed with lime, settled into all the broad valleys that little by little, as the ocean sank, became free of water; and in the middle of them the rivers dug only shallow beds. At that time elephants and rhinoceroses were at home here upon the exposed mountains, and their remains could very easily be washed down by woodland streams into those great stream basins or ocean flats, where, more or less permeated with minerals, they were preserved and where we now dig them up by accident with the plow or in other ways. It is in this sense that I said earlier that one finds them in the upper level, in that, namely, which the old rivers washed together, as the main crust of the earth's surface was already fully formed. Now the time will soon come when one will no longer just throw fossils all together but will classify them according to the world epochs. "

Goethe has repeatedly been called a precursor of the geology founded by Lyell. Geology also no longer assumes mighty revolutions or catastrophes in order to explain how one earth period arises out of another. It traces earlier changes of the earth's surface back to the same processes that are still at work now. But one should also be aware of the fact that modern geology brings forth only physical and chemical forces to explain earth formation. That Goethe, on the other hand, assumes formative forces that are at work within the masses and that represent a higher kind of formative principles than physics and chemistry know.

Observations about Atmospheric Phenomena

In 1815 Goethe becomes acquainted with Luke Howard's *Attempt at a Natural History and Physics of the Clouds*. He is stimulated by it to sharpen his reflection about cloud formations and atmospheric conditions. He had in fact already made many earlier observations about these phenomena and recorded them. But he lacked "overview and branches of science to connect with" in order to bring together what he had experienced. In Howard's essay the manifold cloud formations are traced back to certain basic forms. Goethe now finds entry into meteorology, which until then had remained foreign to him because for his nature it was impossible to gain anything from the way this branch of science was handled in his time. "For my nature it was impossible to grasp the whole complex of meteorology in the way it was set up in tables of numbers and symbols; I was glad to find an integrating part of this science to be in accord with my inclination and life, and, because everything in this endless universe stands in eternal sure relationship, because one thing brings forth the other or is brought forth by it, I sharpened my gaze for what the eyes can grasp and accustomed myself to bring the interconnections of atmospheric and earth phenomena into harmony with the barometer and thermometer..."

Since the level of barometric pressure stands in an exact relationship to all weather conditions, it soon came for Goethe into the center of his observations of atmospheric conditions. The longer he continues these observations the more he believes he recognizes that the rise and fall of mercury in the barometer at different "places of observation, whether they be nearer or farther away or of varying length, breadth, and height," occurs in such a way that for a rise or fall in one place there corresponds an almost equally great rise or fall at all other places at the same time. From this regularity of barometric changes Goethe draws the conclusion that no influences outside the earth can affect these changes. When one ascribes such an influence to the moon, planets, seasons, when one speaks of ebb and flow in the atmosphere, then the regularity is not explained. All these influences would have to manifest themselves at the same time in different places in the most different ways. Only when the cause of these changes lies within the earth itself are they explainable, Goethe believes. Since the level of mercury depends upon atmospheric pressure, Goethe pictures to himself that the earth alternately compresses the whole atmosphere and expands it again. If the air is compressed then its pressure increases and the mercury rises; the opposite occurs with expansion. Goethe ascribes this alternating compression and expansion of the entire mass of air to a changeability to which the earth's force of gravity is subjected. He sees the increase and decrease of this force to be founded in a certain individual life of the earth, and he compares it to the inbreathing and outbreathing of an organism.

In accordance with this Goethe also does not think of the earth as active in a merely *mechanical* way. Just as little as he explains geological processes in a purely mechanical and physical sense does he do so in regard to barometric changes. His view of nature stands in sharp opposition to the modern one. The latter seeks, in accordance with its general basic principles, to grasp atmospheric processes in a physical sense. Differences of temperature in the atmosphere bring about a difference of atmospheric pressure in different places, create air currents from warmer to colder regions, increase or decrease humidity, bring forth cloud formations and precipitation. Out of these and similar factors the variations in atmospheric pressure, and with them the rise and fall of the barometer, are explained. Goethe's picture of an increase and decrease in the force of gravity is also in opposition to modern mechanical concepts. According to them the strength of the force of gravity at any one place is always the same.

Goethe applies mechanical conceptions only to the extent that observation seems to dictate.

V

Goethe and Hegel

Goethe's contemplation of the world goes only to a certain limit. He observes light and color phenomena and advances as far as the archetypal phenomenon *(Urphaenomen);* he tries to find his bearings within the manifoldness of the plant's being and arrives at his sensible-supersensible archetypal plant. From the archetypal phenomenon or the archetypal plant he does not ascend to higher principles of explanation. He leaves that up to the philosophers. He is content when "he finds himself upon the empirical heights, from which he can look back upon experience in all its levels, and can at least look forward into the realm of theory if not enter it." Goethe goes to the point in his contemplation of the real where the ideas confront him. To determine the connection in which ideas stand to one another and how, within, the ideal realm, one thing proceeds from another, are tasks that first begin upon the empirical height where Goethe stopped. "The idea is eternal and unique," he believes. "That we also use the plural is not appropriate. Everything of which we can become aware and about which we can speak are only manifestations of the idea." But since the idea, in the phenomenon, arises after all as a multiplicity of individual ideas, such as idea of the plant, idea of the animal, these must then let themselves be led back to a basic form in the same way that the plant lets itself be led back to the leaf. The individual ideas are also different only in their manifestation; in their true being they are identical. It is therefore just as much in keeping with the Goethean world view to speak of a metamorphosis of ideas as of a metamorphosis of plants. The philosopher who tried to present this metamorphosis of ideas is Hegel. Through this he is the philosopher of the Goethean world view. He takes his start from the simplest idea, from pure "being." Within this being the true shape of world phenomena conceals itself completely. Then rich content becomes a bloodless abstraction. Hegel has been reproached for deriving the whole content-filled world of ideas from pure being. But pure being contains "as idea" the entire world of ideas, just as the leaf contains as idea the entire plant. Hegel follows the metamorphoses of the idea from pure abstract being up to the level at which the idea becomes directly real phenomenon. He considers the phenomenon of philosophy to be this highest level. For, in philosophy, the ideas that are at work in the world are beheld in their own inherent shape. To express this in Goethe's way one could say that philosophy is the idea in its greatest expansion; pure being is the idea in its uttermost contraction. The fact that Hegel sees in philosophy the most complete metamorphosis of the idea shows that true attentiveness to himself is as far removed from him as from Goethe. A thing has attained its highest metamorphosis when it brings forth its full content in perception, in immediate life. But philosophy contains the world's content of ideas not in the form of life but rather in the form of thoughts. The living idea, the idea as perception, is given only to human self-observation. Hegel's philosophy is not a world view of freedom, because it does not seek the world content in its highest form upon the ground of the human personality. On this ground all content becomes entirely individual. Hegel does not seek this individual but rather the general, the genus. For this reason he also does not place the origin of the moral into the human individual but rather into the world order lying outside man that is supposed to contain the moral ideas. The human being does not give himself his own moral goal but rather has to make himself a part of the moral world order. The single, the individual is for Hegel precisely the bad, if it persists in its singleness. Only within the whole does it first receive its value. This is the attitude of the bourgeoisie, Max Stirner asserts, "and its poet, Goethe, like its philosopher, Hegel, knew how to glorify the dependency of the subject upon the object, obedience to the objective world, and so on." There again another one-sided way of picturing things is presented. Hegel, like Goethe, lacks the perception *(Anschauung)* of freedom, because the perception of the innermost being of the thought world escapes them both. Hegel definitely feels himself to be the philosopher of the Goethean world view. On February 20, 1821 he writes to Goethe, "The simple and abstract, what you quite aptly call the archetypal phenomenon, this you put first, and then show the concrete phenomena as arising through the participation of still other influences and circumstances, and you direct the whole process in such a way that the sequence proceeds from the simple determining factors to the composite ones, and, thus arranged, something complex appears in all its clarity through this decomposition. To seek out the archetypal phenomenon, to free it from other extraneous chance surroundings—to grasp it abstractly, as we call it—this I consider to be a task for a great spiritual sense for nature, just as I consider that procedure altogether to be what is truly scientific in gaining knowledge in this field." "...But may I now also still speak to you about the particular interest that the archetypal phenomenon, lifted out in this way, has for us philosophers, namely that we can put such a preparation precisely to philosophical use! If, namely, in spite of everything, we have finally led our initially oysterlike, gray, or completely black absolute out toward the air and light, so that it desires them, then we need windows in order to lead it out fully into the light of day; our schemata would disperse into mist if we were to transfer them directly into the colorful confused society of a resistant world. Here is where your archetypal phenomena now stand us in excellent stead; in this twilight, spiritual and comprehensible through its simplicity, visible or graspable through its sense-perceptibility—the two worlds greet each other: our abstruse existence and the manifest one. "

Even though Goethe's world view and Hegel's philosophy correspond completely to each other, still a person would be quite mistaken if he were to place the same value upon the thought achievements of Goethe and those of Hegel. The same way of picturing things lives in both. Both want to avoid self-perception. But Goethe carried out his reflections in areas in which this lack of perception does not have a harmful effect. Even if he never did see the world of ideas as perception, he did nevertheless *live* in the world of ideas and allowed his observations to be permeated by it. Hegel viewed the world of ideas as perception, as individual spiritual existence, just as little as Goethe did. But he carried out his reflections precisely on the world of ideas. In many directions his reflections are therefore awry and untrue. If Hegel had carried out observations about nature, then they would have become every bit as valuable as those of Goethe; if Goethe had wanted to set up a philosophical thought structure, then that sure view of true reality would certainly have forsaken him that guided him in his considerations of nature.

Epilogue to the New Edition of 1918

It was said by critics of this book immediately after its publication that it does not give a picture of Goethe's "world view" but only of his "view of nature." I do not think that this judgment comes from a justified point of view, even though, looked at externally, the book deals almost exclusively with Goethe's ideas about nature. For I believe that in the course of what has been said I have shown that these ideas about nature rest upon a quite definite way of looking at the phenomena of the world. And in my opinion I have indicated in the book itself that taking a point of view toward the phenomena of nature such as Goethe had can lead to definite views about psychological, historical, and still wider phenomena of the world. What expresses itself in Goethe's view of nature about a particular area is, in fact, a world view, not a mere view of nature that a person could also have whose thoughts have no significance for a wider picture of the world. On the other hand, however, I believed I should not present anything in this book other than what can be said in direct connection with the realm that Goethe himself worked through out of the totality of his world view. To sketch the picture of the world that arises out of Goethe's literary works, out of his ideas on art history, etc. is of course altogether possible and certainly of the greatest possible interest. A person who is attentive to the stance of this book will not, however, seek in it any *such* world picture. Such a person will recognize that I set myself the task of resketching that part of the Goethean world picture for which in his own writings there are statements that emerge in an unbroken sequence from each other. I have indeed also indicated in many places the points at which Goethe got stuck in this unbroken development of his world picture, but that he did successfully achieve in certain realms of nature. Goethe's views about the world and life show themselves to the broadest extent. How these views emerge out of his own particular world view, however, is not observable in his works outside the area of natural phenomena in the same way that it is within this area. In these other areas what Goethe's soul had to manifest to the world becomes observable; in the area of his ideas about nature there becomes visible how the basic impulse of his spirit achieved, step by step, a world view up to a certain boundary. Precisely through the fact that one does not for once go further in sketching Goethe's thought-work than to present what developed within him as a conceptually cohesive part of a world view, light will be shed upon the particular coloration of what otherwise reveals itself in his life's work. Therefore I did not want to paint the picture of the world that speaks out of Goethe's life work as a whole but rather that part that comes to light with him in the form in which one brings a world view to expression in thought. Views that well up in a personality, however great that personality may be, are not yet parts of a world view picture that is cohesive in itself and that the personality himself conceives to be a coherent whole. But Goethe's nature ideas are just such a cohesive part of a world view picture. And, as illumination for natural phenomena, these ideas are not merely a view of nature but rather a part of a *world view*

*

The fact that I have also been reproached with respect to this book for changing my views after its publication does not surprise me since I am not unfamiliar with the presuppositions that move a person to make such judgments. I have expressed myself about this search for contradictions in my books in the preface to the first volume of my *Riddles of Philosophy* and in an article in the journal, *Das Reich* ("Spiritual Science as Anthroposophy and Contemporary Epistemology"). This kind of search is possible only for critics who completely fail to recognize how in fact my world view *must* proceed in order to grasp the different areas of life. I do not want to go into this question in a general way again here but rather will just briefly state a few things about this book on Goethe. I consider the anthroposophically oriented spiritual science that I have been presenting in my books for sixteen years to be a way of knowing the spiritual world content accessible to man; and a person who has enlivened within himself Goethe's ideas on nature as something right for him and, starting there, strives for experiences of knowledge about the spirit realm, must come to this way of knowing. I am of the view that *this* spiritual science presupposes a natural science that corresponds to the Goethean one. I not only mean by this that the spiritual science presented by me does not contradict this natural science. For I know how little it signifies for there to be *only* no logical contradiction between different assertions. In spite of this they could in reality be utterly incompatible. But rather I believe I have insight into the fact that Goethe's ideas about the realm of nature, if really experienced, must necessarily lead to the anthroposophical knowledge presented by me, if a person does something that Goethe did not yet do, that is to lead experiences in the realm of nature over into experiences in the realm of spirit. The nature of these latter experiences is described in my spiritual scientific works. This is the reason for also reprinting now, after the publication of my spiritual scientific books, the essential content of this present book, that I brought out for the first time in 1897, as my recapitulation of the Goethean world view. I consider all the thoughts presented in it to be still valid today, unchanged. I have only in individual places made changes that do not pertain to the configuration of thoughts but only to the style of individual expressions. And the fact that after twenty years one would want to make a few stylistic changes here and there in a book can, after all, seem comprehensible. Otherwise, what is different in the new edition from the previous one are only some expansions, not changes, of the content. I believe that a person who is seeking a natural scientific foundation for spiritual science can find it through Goethe's world view. Therefore it seems to me that a book about Goethe's world view can also be of significance for someone who wants to concern himself with anthroposophically oriented spiritual science. But the stance of my book is that it wants to consider Goethe's world view entirely for itself, *without reference to actual spiritual science.* (One will find in my book, *Goethe's Faust and the Fairy Tale of the Green Snake,* something of what there is to say about Goethe from the particularly spiritual scientific point of view.) *Supplementary note:* A critic of this book of mine on Goethe believed he had found a special trove of "contradictions," when he placed what I say about Platonism in this book (in the first edition of 1897) beside a statement I made at almost exactly the same time in my introduction to volume four of Goethe's natural scientific writings (Kuerschner edition): "The philosophy of Plato is one of the most sublime edifices of thought that has ever sprung from the spirit of mankind. It is one of the saddest signs of our time that the Platonic way of looking at things is regarded in philosophy as the exact opposite of healthy reason." It is indeed difficult for certain minds to grasp that each thing, when looked at from different sides, presents itself differently. It will be easy to see that my different statements about Platonism do not represent any real contradiction to anyone who does not get stuck at the mere sound of the words but who goes into the different relationships into which I had to bring Platonism, through its own being, at this or that time. It is on the one hand a sad sign when Platonism is regarded as going against healthy reason because only that is considered to be in accordance with reason that stays with mere sense perception as the sole reality. And it does go against a healthy view of idea and sense world to change Platonism in such a way that through it an unhealthy separation of idea and sense perception is brought about. Someone who cannot enter into this kind of thinking penetration of the phenomena of life remains, with what he grasps, always outside of reality. Someone—as Goethe expresses it—who plants a concept in the way in order to limit a rich life's content has no sense for the fact that life unfolds in relationships that work differently in different directions. It is more comfortable, to be sure, to set a schematic concept in the place of a view of the fullness of life; with such concepts one can indeed judge easily and schematically. But one lives, through such a process, in abstractions without being. Thus human concepts turn into abstractions, that one believes can be treated in the intellect in the same way that things treat each other. But these concepts are much more like pictures that one receives of a thing from different sides. The thing is one; the pictures are many. And it is not focusing on *one* picture that leads to a view of the thing but rather looking at several pictures together. Unfortunately I now had to see how strongly many critics are inclined to construct contradictions out of such a consideration of a phenomenon from different points of view, which strives to merge with reality. Because of this I felt moved, with respect to the passages on Platonism in this new edition, first of all to change the style of presentation and thus to make even more definite what seemed to me twenty years ago really to be clear enough in the context in which it stands; secondly, by directly placing the statement from my other book *beside* what is said in this book, to show how both statements stand in total harmony with each other. In doing so I have spared anyone who still has a taste for finding contradictions in such things the trouble of having to gather them from two books.

www.ingramcontent.com/pod-product-compliance
Lightning Source LLC
Chambersburg PA
CBHW020200090426
42734CB00008B/895